Finance for Freelancers

How to get started and make sure you get paid

Andrew Holmes

A & C Black • London

First published in Great Britain 2008

A & C Black Publishers Ltd
38 Soho Square, London W1D 3HB
www.acblack.com

Copyright © Andrew Holmes, 2008

The Guardian is a registered trademark of the Guardian Media Group plc.
Guardian Books is an imprint of Guardian Newspapers Ltd.

A CIP record for this book is available from the British Library.

ISBN: 9-781-408-10116-2

This book is produced using paper that is made from wood grown in
managed, sustainable forests. It is natural, renewable and recyclable.
The logging and manufacturing processes conform to the
environmental regulations of the country of origin.

Design by Fiona Pike, Pike Design, Winchester
Typeset by RefineCatch Limited, Bungay, Suffolk
Printed in the United Kingdom by CPI Bookmarque, Croydon

Contents

Preface

This book is about finance, but it's not typical of the books you tend find on an accountant's bookshelf – which are usually deeply technical and full of example balance sheets and profit-and-loss statements (although I do include both here!). This one is about freelancers and the specific financial issues they face. Although it's financially focused, it certainly doesn't fall into the camp of the standard financial texts that are often thrust into your hand when you mention that you're considering setting up your own business – or at least I hope it doesn't. I've known many freelancers in my time and the one thing I've noticed about them is how disinterested, and even uninterested, they are in finance. Of course, the same is true for anyone who's not an accountant, but the need to be financially literate is possibly more important for a freelancer and ignorance can be very costly.

When Lisa Carden of A & C Black asked if I would write a book on the topic, I thought it was a great idea and one which hopefully will benefit a wide range of people – both those considering going freelance and those who are already pursuing their own interests outside mainstream employment. When I mentioned that I was about to embark on the book to my many freelance friends and colleagues, the response was overwhelmingly positive. Everyone thought it was about time and many believed they would have benefited from such a book years ago, when they first made the move to go freelance. Even my accountant thought it was a super idea, so I just hope that this book hits the mark. To make it as useful as possible, I've drawn on a range of sources which includes existing freelancers who've faced many of the financial issues I discuss. I hope you find it helpful, practical and informative, whether you're considering a freelance career or are already out there toughing it out in the ever-increasingly competitive marketplace in which so many of us are trying to survive and prosper.

Acknowledgements

As with all my books, there are people to whom I am indebted. So, in no particular order, I would like to thank James McColl, until very recently a long-term freelancer; David Jacobs, who has toughed it out in the world of IT for as long as I can remember; Kevin Fitzpatrick, my accountant, who keeps me on top of the many tax and accounting issues that I need to be aware of as a freelance; Nick Birks of Her Majesty's Revenue and Customs, who has always taken an interest in my writing; and Lindsey Simpson, a freelance PR and internal communications consultant, who was kind enough to read the finished manuscript and offer some very helpful input. And finally to Sally, Tom and Libby, who have become so used to me writing that that they no longer ask what I am writing about!

About the author

Andrew Holmes is a writer, management consultant and Managing Partner of Paricint LLP. He has consulted with many household names in the UK and overseas and has written 16 books on a range of business topics as well as non-fiction and humour titles. He lives in Hampshire with his wife and two children.

Introduction: The rise of the freelancer

In the second half of the twentieth century, the key to understanding America's social and economic life was the organisational man. In the first half of the twenty-first century, the new emblematic figure is the free agent – the independent worker who operates on his or her own terms, untethered to a large organisation, serving multiple clients and customers instead of a single boss.[1]

Freelance workers are those who pursue their own professional calling without any long-term commitment to a single employer. Although the concept of freelance work has been with us for many years in various guises, the term is surprisingly a relatively recent one. According to some sources, it was first coined by Sir Walter Scott, who wrote about a medieval mercenary – or 'free-lance' – in his novel *Ivanhoe*. Indeed, selling your military skills to the highest bidder was something our medieval ancestors did very well, although finding yourself on the wrong side often proved to be fatal. Since then, 'freelance' has become a

[1] Pink, D. (2001), *Free Agent Nation*, New York: Warner Books, p. 25

familiar term to describe someone who is willing to sell his or her skills to anyone happy to buy them.

Freelance work is particularly popular within certain professions including journalism, writing, consulting, accountancy, computer programming and graphic design, and of course the military. As a career choice, freelancing is increasingly popular and freelancers represent a significant proportion of the working population of most modern economies. For example, in the United States, there are approximately 10.3 million independent contractors, representing around 7.4 per cent of the American workforce. In the UK, there are around 3.8 million sole traders (including partners like myself) who can be considered self-employed, or freelancers.

There's a strong indication, then, that there are plenty of people who are willing to take a risk and work under their own direction, rather than for an employer. The number of freelancers is on the rise, too, and this growth has been fuelled by various technical, organisational and social trends. Some of the main ones are:

■ the end of the concept of a 'job for life'. In the late 1990s, the much-touted business acronym BPR – business process re-engineering (in other words, downsizing) – destroyed the concept of a 'psychological contract' between workers and their employer. The notion that employees would work hard and keep their noses clean in return for a safe and secure career fell apart as workers were sacked in droves under the 'don't automate, obliterate' mantra of BPR experts and consultants. Employees quickly cottoned on the fact that they could no longer depend on their bosses to look after them and honour their part of the bargain; they'd need to look out for themselves from now on. As a result, many people – and especially those with transferable skills and expertise – have decided to take the plunge, place themselves on the open market and work with those organisations who are willing to pay well for their services.

- the increasing importance of 'knowledge work'. such as computing, market research, consultancy and other types of work which requires the use of our brains rather than our physical capabilities. As Western economies shed their manufacturing industries in favour of service industries and the impact of technological advances been felt, there has been a general shift away from blue-collar work. Unlike working on a production line in a factory, there's no real need for employees to be tied to the workplace; knowledge work has no physical boundaries and, as such, makes it possible for people to work from wherever they like.

- the increasing number of companies who outsource a lot of their administrative and less valuable work. Although Henry Ford and others used this to access local markets during the 1920s and 30s, it took off as trend only really as the year 2000 grew closer and when the much-feared Millennium Bug loomed large in many IT directors' minds.

Companies around the world offshored the remediation work necessary to update the millions of computer systems that could have been affected. Since then, companies have continued to expand the outsourcing and offshoring of jobs.

- the ability to remain connected to clients and colleagues through a combination of reliable PCs and laptops, high-speed broadband wireless networks, and increasingly, the ubiquitous (and for some, addictive) BlackBerry.

- the increasing significance of the Internet. Being able to sell and promote services online has been a boon to us all; these days we can buy pretty much whatever we want, wherever we want, and gain access to products and services that previously would have been difficult or even impossible to source.

Each of these individual changes has had an effect, but it's their collective impact that has made the freelance option increasingly viable for so many of us.

Perhaps the one thing freelancers have to consider more than anything else has nothing to do with how good they are, or what skills and expertise they bring to the party, but has everything to do with the financial aspects of what they do; it's about getting paid, keeping solvent and building a long-term future. And that's the purpose of this book. It aims to provide anyone who's currently freelance, or who may be considering a freelance career,

with a clear understanding of why finance is important.
It addresses:

- the financial considerations before moving into freelance work
- the financial implications of how you choose to structure your business
- the basic financial competences you'll need
- how to maximise the value – and hence income – from your venture
- how to source your work
- some basics on invoicing and debt management
- avoiding some of the many financial pitfalls associated with freelance work
- the need to consider your tax position
- keeping money aside for a rainy day and thinking about your long-term financial stability
- establishing a path of long-term growth

I hope you'll find this a useful, informative and helpful guide as you navigate the financial challenges all freelancers need to think about.

Taking the plunge

Many of us dream about working for ourselves, no longer shackled to a corporate desk with the freedom to work when, how and where we like. Of course, dreaming is what most people end up doing, as the perceived risks associated with going it alone can be daunting enough to put off anyone. Let's face it, cutting free from any employer can be difficult and this is doubly hard for those of us who work for large companies. All of the reasons why you might want to leave – perhaps the boredom, the annoying colleagues or appalling boss – usually pale into insignificance when you consider the biggest obstacle of all: finance. The loss of a steady pay cheque at the end of the month, the pension contributions (well not so great these days, but many employers still offer something and some, like the civil service, can be especially generous), the paid holiday, the sick leave if you need it and all the overheads paid for – all these serve to make the decision a difficult one. I know what it feels like.

The leap of faith

In 2007, I sat over my laptop constructing my resignation letter. At the time I was working for PricewaterhouseCoopers, the largest of the Big Four multidisciplinary professional services firms. I was doing well enough and could have toughed it out until I retired, but the prospect of doing so just didn't excite me and, in any case, I would have stagnated, got bored and then moved on anyway, albeit a few years later. I'd thought about leaving for at least six months and during this time considered my options carefully, as I wasn't in any tearing hurry. I could, of course, have stayed, but I felt that was out of the question. I could have joined another firm doing similar work and facing the same kinds of issues but with a different company name on my business card. Or I could have gone back into industry. But even that failed to excite me because I guess I'd become so used to working on different projects with a range of clients across business sectors that working for a single company might prove to be a problem further down the line. I'd explored the possibility of becoming a chief executive for a London law firm, for example, but even then, I felt that turning up at the same office, day after day, would soon lose its appeal. In the end, freelancing was possibly the best way forward. So a few months after my first deliberations, there I was crafting the letter very carefully, agonising over every word. And, as I wrote it, all the 'what-if' questions crowded my brain:

- What if I can't find enough work to replace my salary?
- What about my pension? What if I can't save enough?
- What about holidays? Will I ever take them again?
- What about my tax position?

As the questions mounted, so did the doubts; the easy option of staying put looked all the more appealing. But I finished my letter, and as my wife came into the room, and saw me sitting there, finger poised over the e-mail send button, she told me that it was now or never. She was right, if I didn't do it now, then I never would and she for one didn't want me to regret not having made the move. So I hit 'send'.

Taking this step reminded me of the film *Indiana Jones and the Last Crusade* (bear with me). With his father mortally wounded, Indiana had no choice but to retrieve the Holy Grail which would save his father and in doing so provide their captors with everlasting life. As he passed through (and survived) the various trials on the way to securing the goblet, he came to the one that was seemingly the most difficult to pass – the leap of faith. As he stood on the edge of a precipice, he could see the tunnel which led to the Grail on the other side. Too far to jump and with no obvious means of propelling himself across the bottomless ravine, his right leg hovered over the edge for what seemed like an age before he finally took a deep breath and allowed his foot to fall. To his relief, a rock bridge appeared beneath his step, and with a firm basis for moving forward, Indiana was able to retrieve the Holy Grail, save his father and escape the villains.

Apart from people like me who've decided to cut ties with their employers, there are plenty of other reasons why people choose to pursue a freelance career. Some are naturally made for it and bypass the employer thing altogether. Others, such as young mothers, choose to freelance because it suits their need to balance childcare with a career. And there are also those who fall into freelance work because they've been made redundant. In such circumstances, it can be the push that they needed, and can lead to a successful future. I've heard plenty of stories of how, following redundancy, people from all walks of life have carved out a successful solo career and only wish they'd done it sooner. Indeed, this is something my father did while I was still very young.

Finally, for those unwilling to take the leap of faith, it's possible to freelance while still working. This avenue is becoming increasingly popular as individuals seek alternatives ways to earn extra income on top of their salary. Although it's possible to earn some additional money doing part-time work, the advantage of pursuing the freelance route is that it allows you to continue to build your career by utilising the skills you've developed so far. For instance, I've been writing for a number of years on a range of topics which are related to my day-to-day activities. But even now my writing career is in addition to my day job. What has made this so effective is that it allows me to explore new ideas I have while working and provides me with an important marketing tool when dealing with my clients. So, although this doesn't provide me with a massive income, it does allow me to increase my market value. It has also taught me some invaluable lessons about how to freelance and some of the financial considerations I needed to be aware of.

Again, for those who want to experience freelance work, but don't feel able, or are perhaps unwilling to be totally alone, there's the option for working for an agency. In this instance the agency will source work for you and in some cases you will be on their books as an employee. Recent changes to the tax legislation, known as IR35, mean that if you work for a single company as a freelancer you are, to all and intents and purposes, an employee and are therefore treated as such by Her Majesty's Revenue & Customs (HMRC). Given the tax implications it is important to understand how you may be affected (see Chapter 8).

Attributes of a successful freelancer

Although many of us feel we could be suited to freelance work, none of us quite knows whether that's true until we've experienced it. So it's worth considering the psychological make-up of a successful freelancer, as this provides a yardstick against which to measure our own suitability. According to various commentators on this type of work, successful solo employees tend to be:

- **SELF-STARTERS.** The one thing you have to be is self-motivated. If you're someone who needs direction and guidance in order to get things done, or requires the occasional kick up the backside, then you may find that you're better off working for someone who'll provide the extrinsic motivation you need. If on the other hand, you're intrinsically motivated and are able to get things done without supervision, then you'll be more suited to freelancing.

- **COMPLETER/FINISHERS.** As the name suggests, this role involves getting things done, having an eye for the detail and keeping everything on track. When you consider the primary reason why organisations employ freelance staff is to get things done, you can see why this skill is so critical.

■ **RESILIENT.** Although it could be argued that anyone working in the same organisation year after year demonstrates a degree of resilience, it's the freelancer who needs it in spades. There's no doubt that freelance work provides freedom from the typical nine-to-five existence, but there comes with this freedom the need to cope with the uncertainty of not always having a steady income stream (for more on how to address this particular issue, see Chapter 5). When there's less money coming in, it's tempting to throw in the towel and re-enter the mainstream employment market, but true freelancers will have the resilience and self-assuredness to continue along their chosen path.

■ **EGOLESS.** Surprising though this may sound, having low ego needs is an essential part of being a successful freelancer. Ego in this sense should not be confused with having a powerful sense of self-worth which is equally important (see the next point, below). Working as a hired hand in different organisations usually means playing second fiddle to someone else's tune rather than your own. Naturally it will depend upon why you've been hired in the first place, as there are occasions where you may be working in a position of relative power (which is what many interim managers do, for example). For the most part, however, you'll need to use your influencing skills to get things done. Leaving your ego at the door is necessary because you need to be able to blend in and become part of the team and organisation in which you'll be working (see the point on being culturally intelligent, below). It's also important to remember that you'll usually be regarded as an outsider and therefore treated differently from full-time employees. Irrespective of whether you feel this is wrong or unfair, it's the reality of freelance work, and is something I learnt very early on in my consulting career, which in my mind is glorified freelancing anyway.

- **SELF-CONFIDENT.** This goes hand-in-hand with being resilient in that it's important to know what you're worth and what skills and capabilities you bring to your clients. This can have a major impact on your financial health, especially when it comes to negotiating deals and getting the rate that you deserve rather than only what the client is willing to pay

- **CULTURALLY INTELLIGENT.** For those in the freelance community who work for a variety of different companies and also overseas, the ability to tune into the culture of the client is also a key skill. Each organisation is different and is likely to have slightly different ways of doing things and defining what is and isn't acceptable. Understanding what makes the organisation in which you're working tick is helpful because it ensures you rapidly become part of the wider team you have to work and get along with. And if you can do this, you'll become accepted, perceived to be dependable and will be able to establish long-term relationships with the companies you work for.

■ **DISCIPLINED.** This is possibly one of the most critical dimensions of success and is not the same as being a self-starter or a completer finisher. The issue here is the discipline that comes with effective and comprehensive record-keeping and managing your finances in terms of billing, debt management and so on. Moving from an environment where you may have had secretarial support to one where there is none leaves a void which for some can be difficult to address. Naturally the ability to keep good records varies and if you're someone who's not good at it, then either you'll need to learn, or you'll have to find someone to do it for you.

Casting your eye over this list and making an honest assessment of how you measure up against these attributes is a good way of determining whether you're suited to freelance work. If you've got these attributes then it's likely that you'll be able to survive the freelance world and make a good living – because the capabilities listed above will impact on such things as sourcing work, keeping on top of your finances and maintaining your motivation. However, if you find that you've only a few of these qualities, you might want to take a different path and either consider remaining in full-time employment, or perhaps begin freelancing while working, as I did when I started my writing career some eight years ago.

Lining up the ducks

Apart from assessing yourself against the attributes of an effective and successful freelancer, the other important activity before taking the plunge is to line up the ducks to ensure you're making the right decision. As already mentioned, not everyone is suited to freelance work and to help you arrive at the right decision it's important to consider the following:

- your motives for freelancing;
- understanding what you're giving up and what you're gaining;
- how financially prepared you are;
- your income expectations and how realistic they are.

Let's explore each of these in turn.

Your motives for freelancing

These are more important than you might think and it's essential that you really understand why you want to freelance. Some people do so because it gives them more free time which they can spend with their family, friends or pursuing other interests which they find more fulfilling, such as the consultant I know who funds her love of skiing through her consulting work. Or freelance friends of mine who work for six months of the year and take the rest of the time off to travel, run marathons and so on. For others, freelancing provides them with the opportunity to develop and grow a business and to be in control of their own destiny. This may, for example, allow them to pursue a particular idea or innovation that wouldn't have been possible within their existing employer. Some like to be free of office politics and to focus on what they're good at, unencumbered by the need to be part of a political system which neither values them nor the skills and capabilities they bring. Then there are those who see freelancing as an opportunity to maximise their income and to sell their skills and capabilities on the open market. Many in the expatriate community aim to do just this; they'll spend the majority of their working life overseas, such as in the Middle East, where their income is tax free.

There are, of course, many other reasons why people choose to freelance, and irrespective of the choice, there are financial implications. Given that it's the financial considerations that cause many of us to have second

11

thoughts about going it alone, and indeed results in many disappointments and failures, it's important to assess these carefully before taking the plunge (more on this later). However, you need to get to the heart of why you want to carve out your own niche, as if you're passionate enough, practical enough and believe in yourself, the financial niggles that would prevent you from taking that bold step can be overcome. Whenever I'm doubtful about whether or not I've made the right move, I look at one of my favourite quotes from Eric Berne, the author of *Games People Play*: 'Many a man with the chemistry of a great ballet dancer spends his time dancing with other people's dishes in a lunchroom, and others with genes of a mathematician pass their days juggling other people's papers in the back room of a bank or bookie joint. But within his chemical limitations, whatever they are, each man has enormous possibilities for determining his own fate.' Now if that's not motivational enough, then I don't know what is.

Understanding what you're giving up and what you're gaining

Having understood why you want to go it alone, it's important that you recognise the consequences of your decision from both a financial and a non-financial perspective. As mentioned earlier, although many of us harbour desires to do our own thing, the pull of the organisation – especially in terms of its perceived financial stability – is enough to put off the majority of us. But, of course, we have to remember that it's more than just a question of the finances, as if it was just a financial matter then many of us would never leave the confines of our employers. Assessing the consequences of making the move to a freelance existence is best done in a methodical and logical way. It's also important to understand your emotional needs and abilities, as these play a key part of the decision-making process, otherwise decisions that add up on paper may not hold true in real life.

I believe the best way to make this assessment is first to draw up a table which consists of three columns. The first identifies the key elements of your current job or career, such as paid holidays; the second captures whether or not the elements identified in the first column apply to your current situation; and the final column highlights whether they will apply to your proposed freelance career. Below is the table I created when I was considering my options. Note that I assessed quite a few non-financial aspects of my situation.

Aspect	Current situation	Future situation
Steady employment	✓	✓
Paid holidays	✓	✗
Interesting clients and projects	✓	✓
Private healthcare/Health insurance	✓	✗
Car allowance	✓	✗
Pension contributions	✓	✗
Opportunity to grow my own business	✗	✓
Opportunity to work with the clients I want	✗	✓
Long-term financial growth opportunities	✗	✓
Opportunity to create something new	✗	✓
Improved work–life balance	✗	✓
Opportunity to work on projects I like	✓	✓
Intellectual freedom	✗	✓
Chance to expand my writing career	✗	✓
Opportunity to expand my academic ties	✗	✓

What's useful about creating a table such as the one above is that it brings out quite starkly the classic intrinsic and extrinsic motivators that people are taught in management 101 courses. The extrinsic motivators, such as the money, the car, the pension etc., are powerful attractors for us all, and especially as you get older when you've an increasing number of pulls on your income, such as kids, saving for retirement and so on. But it is the non-financial factors, such as the opportunity to grow intellectually, or the chance to be in charge of your own destiny which truly define us, and more importantly, excite us. So although we all need to earn enough of an income to maintain our chosen lifestyles, it's the intrinsic motivators that get us out of bed in the morning. The other thing to note is that many of these intrinsic aspects can have a financial outcome. Think about running your own business, or the chance to create something new; each of these will, over time, have an impact financially, and of course you'll be more passionate about them and hence more likely to succeed. Creating a table of what you'll gain and what you'll lose will, at the very least, allow you to take a dispassionate look at what's likely to motivate you to take the plunge. And, if it helps, you might want to prioritise your list so that you can see what the principal drivers are for you.

Many people tell me that, when considering the option to move into self-employment, it's also helpful to consider what are known as 'day in the life of scenarios'. Day in the life of scenarios are typically a way of assessing an employee's productivity and are used to identify those time sinks which can be avoided with a bit more planning, focus and concentration. The reason why they can be helpful from a freelance perspective is that they allow you to walk through what your typical day would be (or how you would like it to be) and from this determine whether freelance work is right for you. One freelance marketer discussed how lonely she was when she first started working for herself; she found the isolation of working from home too much, so she redesigned her approach to work to increase the amount of time she spent working on projects on site with her clients, rather than remotely. And not surprisingly, she started to enjoy her freelance life a lot more. (The subtext here is that it's important to remember that you can design your work to suit your needs.)

As with the table of what you'll gain and lose with the move to freelancing, it can also be helpful to compare your current day in the life and that of your new working environment as a freelancer. Below is a simple example of a day in the life of a corporate lawyer, which – although it may not directly relate to what you currently do, or would like to – will give you a sense of the level of detail you might need to go into. The one thing this example tells me is that I wouldn't want to become a lawyer; I know a few and they work very, very long hours. Completing a day in the life for your future freelance role will allow you to appreciate if you'll cope with the possible isolation and assess whether or not you prefer the structure and control that a corporate timetable brings. Let's face it, some of us find it liberating, while others crippling. If you find that you prefer the corporate life, then freelancing might not be for you.

EXAMPLE DAY IN THE LIFE OF A CORPORATE LAWYER

08.45 Check voice mail and e-mail

10.00 Arrive at office; check voice mail and e-mail; receive call from Client B regarding an agreement that needs to be drafted relating to a deal that was recently closed

10.15 Receive call from Client C regarding new deal

10.45 Conduct conflicts search with respect to new target company for Client C

10.50 Receive call from associate regarding questions related to preparation of organisational documents for a start-up company (Client D)

11.00 Review draft of investment agreement for Client C

13.15 Contact senior and mid-level associates to staff transaction for Client C; brief associates on background, timing and key points of deal

13.30 Order lunch and eat at desk while continuing to review investment agreement

13.45 Receive call from Client C; discuss significant deal points on new transaction

14.30 Conduct Internet research on potential new client in preparation for a lunch meeting with a potential new client the following day

14.45 Meeting with associates regarding investment document related to new transaction for Client C

15.00 Begin to review revised equity documents (shareholders agreement, stock purchase agreement, registration rights agreement, charter and bylaws)

16.00 Receive call from opposing counsel on matter for Client A; 16:00 conference call delayed to 17.15

16.10 Client D (start-up company) calls with two of its founders

16.45 Receive call from Client B regarding changes in required letter agreement

16.50 Call associate on matter for Client B to confirm that associate is drafting agreement and discuss points raised by client

17.15 Conference call begins with opposing counsel on matter for Client A

18.25 Call ends. Conference call with associate and Client A to discuss open points in equity documents

18.40 Call senior associate on matter for Client C regarding impending meeting

18.45 Review draft letter agreement for Client B

19.00 Prepare for meeting and leave office with colleague to go to opposing counsel's office on matter for Client C

19.05 Meeting with client, lead investor and lead investor's counsel. Discuss and resolve several of the significant business issues

20.30 Client C leaves; with colleague continue to negotiate with lead investor's counsel regarding the remaining business and legal issues in the document

21.50 Receive call from Client C

22.10 With colleague, meet counsel for lead investor

22.30 Car home. Check voice mail

22.45 Arrive home. Check e-mail. Respond to e-mails

23.15 Go to bed

How financially prepared you are

When you consider how many people generally fail to manage their finances properly, you can begin to understand why a number of freelancers get into financial difficulties. Living from monthly pay cheque to monthly pay cheque is a reality for a significant percentage of the working population (as high as 50 per cent according to some commentators) and in plenty of cases it's because no one pays attention to what's leaving their bank account. Very few people either create, or live within, a defined budget. When you've a steady income coming in from your employer, the ability to budget is relatively straightforward and all that it requires to keep on top of things is to keep your spending within the limits of your income. Added to this, an increasing number of employees receive a bonus, which can come in very handy at the end of the year and especially when you may have spent more than you've earned.

The problem when you're a freelancer is that you may not have the steady income that you have learnt to live with while in full-time employment, so it's imperative that you review your finances to assess how prepared you are. In other words, it's essential that you enter the freelance world with your financial eyes wide open, as I've seen quite a few freelancers get into financial difficulty simply because they've failed to understand where their money goes.

The best way to assess your financial preparedness is to review your monthly expenditure by identifying the principal areas where you spend money. My starter for ten would be:

- mortgage or rent
- food and general housekeeping expenses
- car (wear and tear and petrol)
- utilities, including gas, electricity, water and telecoms
- council tax
- loans and credit card debt

- clothing
- If you've a family, childcare and schooling which should include such things as private school fees (if appropriate), university tuition fees, field trips, bus service, dinners, uniforms and so on (even small school expenses soon add up)
- insurance – including car, travel and home insurance
- personal insurance and protection – including endowments, critical illness cover, life cover and so on
- pension contributions
- travel to work expenses
- television licence
- child maintenance/CSA payments
- entertainment costs which can include eating out, trips out, holidays, cinema, social drinking etc.

As a list, this is a good enough start and you might want to make an estimate of the other one-off expenses that crop up during a typical year, such as repairs to your car and home, as these can be pretty expensive and when they're unplanned for they can be quite unsettling. Once you've completed this exercise, you'll have a good understanding of what your day-to-day living expenses are. You then need to roll the monthly figure to an annual amount, as this is likely to be the baseline of the earnings you'd like to achieve.

As part of your assessment of how financially prepared you are, you'll need to consider a small number of other things, such as:

▓ any savings you might have which you could draw on as you start your freelance career. Ideally, these should be as accessible as possible, such as in a building society or Individual Savings Account (ISA). Naturally you have to be careful not to deplete all your surplus money, as you might need to tap into it later on.

▓ what lines of credit could be available to you, should you require them. For example, the number of freelancers and entrepreneurs has increased along with house prices for the simple reason that it's been possible to fund a start-up business from the equity tied up in their property. This trend also works in reverse when house prices stagnate or fall too, so it's clear that less liquid funds are just as an important source of initial finance as cash. You can also seek funding from your local bank, but here you'll need a detailed business plan to support any loan you might need. If you're going to take out a loan, you might want to check your credit record as your score will impact the interest rate you pay. You can check your credit score with someone like Experian (www.experian.co.uk).

While it's vital that you have a clear understanding of your current financial position before you move into freelancing, if you want to be really prepared, you might also want to think about those areas of spending you could possibly rein in if necessary. As a general rule, I pay for as much as possible using direct debits and standing orders, as in this way, I know exactly what goes out of my account every month (the important things that is), and how much surplus I have to spend. So if I have a tougher month, I know what the absolute minimum is I need to get paid. After that, it's extra for spending and of course saving (there's more on this topic in Chapter 9).

Your income expectations and how realistic they are

Having assessed your finances in general, you then need to consider two more things. The first is to think about your income expectations. Irrespective of your underlying motives for moving into freelance employment, you still need to be paid and it's important to think about how much income you want when you first start out and how this might change as your freelance career continues. Having reviewed your finances you'll have a clear idea about how much income you need to maintain your current living standards. And that's just the start.

It never ceases to amaze me just how many freelancers aren't commercially minded. A large number move into freelance work without fully understanding what they're worth, or how to negotiate a good deal (for them and their clients). Being commercially minded is important if you want to maximise your income, but you also have to be realistic. Like everything else, it's worth doing your research before you seek out your first contract. So it's a good idea to speak to agents who source work for contractors, talk to other freelancers you might know and do a little bit of research on the Web. If you cast your net wide enough, you'll be able to get a sense of the range of daily, hourly, and project-based rates available and then consider what rates you might be able to achieve. From my personal experience of working with major consulting houses, I had a good understanding of what rates I could earn, and this certainly helped when I negotiated my first contract. You have to be realistic though, because although you don't want to undersell yourself, you also don't want to price yourself out of the market, unless you're willing to walk away from work. That said, I know many freelancers who'll deliberately try to price themselves out of a job they don't want to do, and are often surprised when the client is willing to pay! So sometimes it pays off to price yourself high; if nothing else it helps you to test your market worth, and if you didn't want the work anyway, you've nothing to lose. Of course, if the client is willing to pay a premium, you may well take the contract anyway. (For more on the topic of getting the value you deserve, see Chapter 4.)

The second thing to consider is your potential profits, and I am assuming that you want to make some. As a rule of thumb, you should be aiming to make anywhere between 10 and 30 per cent profit on your turnover (which is not the same as profit – see Chapter 3). The actual figure will vary according to the type of work you do. So in very simple terms, your turnover (how much you want to earn in a typical year) needs to cover your day-to-day living expenses as identified above plus your profit.

Coping with the transition

Moving into freelance work isn't easy, and it's essential to remember that it takes time to get used to it. Keep this in mind if you become plagued by a whole range of feelings including self-doubt, worries about where the next contract is coming from, or how you'll be able to keep working as a freelancer for a period of years. These are quite natural concerns but you have to counter them with the good things which come from moving into freelance employment, such as a real sense of control, freedom to choose what you do, the improved balance in your life and so on. The best advice I received from a contractor friend of mine – and an attitude that's been reinforced as I've read around the subject – was to view the move to freelance employment just like any other change in job, company or career. And I think he's right. Over the course of my career, I've worked for many different companies, changed role numerous times, picked up new responsibilities and embraced new challenges. In each instance, I've gone through very similar emotions as I did when I moved into a freelance environment – in fact most of the ones I've listed above.

Time and the effort required to be successful are two additional considerations to take into account. According to the advice of career counsellors, shifting career takes a lot of work and may require building new skills and capabilities and perhaps even intensive networking. Unfortunately, many people lack the stamina unless they lay the necessary groundwork. Time is also key, as many fail to understand just how long it can take to settle into a new career or role; indeed, most of us tend to underestimate this considerably, which is why a lot of us give up and move back into mainstream employment. When I reflect on the changes I've made over my career, it took me somewhere between six and 18 months before I truly settled into a new role, position, employer or career. Freelancing is no different; you have to give it time.

Taking the plunge requires you to conquer your fears and having decided to make that all-important move, the next thing is to decide on how to structure your freelance role or company. As you'd expect, there are quite a few choices when you're setting up your own company and each of these has a financial implication, which will be reviewed in the next chapter.

First things first: Choosing your company's structure

Before you make the leap to freelance work, the first thing you need to do is to consider how you want to structure your company and of course what you want to call it. Like so many things in life, there are choices and these will have an impact on what you might earn, how much you might end up paying in taxes and how your company will grow. Ideally, you want to use a structure which gives you the best of all worlds and one in which you can maximise your income, minimise your tax and build your company.

Naming your business

Before reviewing the legal structures you can choose from, it's worth making a brief departure to discuss what to call your company. Although selecting a name for your company is probably one of the most important decisions you'll make, many small businesses fail to give it sufficient thought. And unfortunately a poor choice at this stage can have major implications later on, not least lost sales and reduced revenue. A company name has to stand out from the crowd, be memorable and easy to find online. If it doesn't do all of these things, it'll be difficult for you to stand out from the competition.

It's easy and often seductive to name a company after yourself. After all, what better way to tell everyone that you're now working under your own steam? Unfortunately, your name implies that it is only you and even if you decide to add 'Associates' after your name, it still looks as though it's really just you with perhaps a couple of friends. Now that may not be a problem: if you simply want to work for yourself and rely exclusively on your personal reputation rather than focus on growing your company into anything more substantial, naming the business after yourself is perhaps not a bad idea. But if you want to create a broader brand, build the company into something more significant and widen the scope of what your business does, then you might want to consider an alternative. This will give you greater flexibility and market presence in the long run. The other problem with using your own name is that if the business does eventually grow into something more significant and you decided to sell it as an ongoing concern, you may end up having to sell your name alongside it, which is what happened to David Lloyd Leisure. This, as you can imagine, can be a bit of a blow.

So to help you avoid a major pitfall, here are some guidelines.

- Your company name should capture the unique value or service you are offering, for example Peterson's Copy Editing Services.
- Don't make the name too obscure or clients will struggle to understand what you are offering.
- Try out a few names first on trusted friends or advisers to see how they react to the name. This will give you some sense of how well it will be received and whether it conjures up an image of what the company is all about. If it does, that's great confirmation, and if it doesn't you know you need to re-think sharpish.
- Check to see whether the relevant domain name is available before you make the final decision (see below).

When considering what you're going to call your company, you'll need to make a few checks to ensure no one else has used it and, increasingly, to see if the website is available. Apart from checking with Companies House (www.companieshouse.gov.uk) or, if you have one, an accountant who'll be able to complete the search for you, it's a good idea to search the Internet to see if there are companies elsewhere with the name you want and although they may not exist in the UK, whether they have the web address that you want. Registering your domain name is straightforward and is best done through one of the many companies that offer a registration service (for example, see www.register.com). The process is very similar to using Companies House to register your company, although without all the paperwork! Once you have found a suitable name, registration takes 24 hours and costs approximately £10, and you will have to pay a similar amount every year to maintain it. Having registered the web address you will need to consider such things as who will host your website. Again, there are plenty of companies who will do this for you and the price of hosting depends on the amount of traffic your website will have, but this is usually between £50–100 per annum.

Company structures

There are five basic legal structures you can opt for when setting up your company and you need to consider the implications of each before arriving at the one that's most suited for you. At this stage, it's a good idea to engage an accountant if you don't already have one, as they can be a great help. The same is true of the major banks that have small business units which can help you navigate through the various decisions you have to make.

The five legal structures are:

1 sole trader
2 limited liability company
3 partnership
4 limited liability partnership
5 franchise

Each of the structures has financial and non-financial implications and the principal differences are explained below. (There's also a table at the end of the chapter which summarises and compares each.) Irrespective of which legal structure you opt for, it's always a good idea to seek expert input from a business adviser, such as Business Link (www.businesslink.gov.uk) or an accountant.

Sole trader

The sole-trader option is possibly the simplest of the structures you can choose, but due to recent changes in the way freelance employees are treated for tax purposes, some of the financial advantages and flexibility which come with being a sole trader have reduced significantly – more on this below. As the name implies, the sole trader is just that: it is you alone selling yourself and your services to your clients. Adopting this approach for freelance work has a range of advantages, the most important being that it gives you complete flexibility on how you choose to manage the business.

From a financial perspective, this option is very simple and doesn't require much in the way of set-up costs; there are no registration fees to pay and record-keeping is very simple. You may need some capital to support you when you first start out which may require a bank loan or – as many freelancers have done when house prices have been buoyant – dipping into the equity within your primary asset. Many sole traders can set up at little or no cost, and this is especially true of the freelance consultant who only really needs a laptop and a mobile phone these days. You'll need to register with HMRC as being self-employed and you'll need to complete an annual tax return (self-assessment) so that your tax can be assessed – remember that you'll no longer fall under the pay as you earn (PAYE) regime you may have been used to. As with any of the options, record-keeping is important and you'll need to keep a note of your income and expenditure. You'll also be liable for National Insurance contributions (NICs), although the amount due will be less than if you were a full-time employee.

The biggest downside of opting for the sole-trader structure is your liability if something goes wrong in the business. As a sole trader, you are personally responsible for any debts you may run up. So if your business gets into difficulties and ends up owing a large amount of money, you may have to sell your assets, including your property if you have any, to pay your creditors. Much, of course, depends on the nature of your business and the likelihood that that you'll run into problems down the line. So although you've greater flexibility under this structure, you do need to be aware of the potential financial downside.

Note that there have recently been key changes to how the self-employed are treated from a tax perspective, as this will have an impact on which legal structure you choose. The most important change to how sole traders are treated is IR35 (more on this in Chapter 8). Under IR35, freelance consultants who've been working for a single client (or an agency, if you use one) for an extended period of time are no longer viewed as being genuinely freelance and are instead treated as employees of the client (or agency). As such, they're bound by the same rules as any other employee. This means that income has to have tax deducted at source by the client (as with every other employee) and in terms of NICs the client has to pay the employer's rate and the sole trader the employee's rate.

As a result, many large organisations now prefer not to engage sole-traders because it not only increases the administrative burden of employing them – thereby negating the flexibility that comes with engaging freelance workers – but it also potentially ends up costing them more. Unsurprisingly, those employing freelance consultants and contractors have either encouraged them to establish a limited company or have gone their separate ways. So if you decide on the sole-trader structure, you just need to be aware of the pitfalls of working with a single client. Long gone are the days when friends of mine could work for many, many years (sometimes well over 10) with the same company earning substantial sums and yet probably indistinguishable from full-time workers. In some cases, they even outlasted them.

Limited liability company

Although setting up a limited company is more involved than being a sole trader and places additional responsibilities on its directors, it makes sense for many freelancers to adopt this structure. It's possible, for example, to buy a company name off the shelf which can reduce some of the administrative burden of setting up a new business. In this instance, a company might have gone bust, or was set up as a dormant business which never traded. Once they cease to trade, it is possible to buy the name of the shelf; remember to check with your accountant or Companies House. The fundamental difference between this and the sole-trader option is that the company exists in its own right and, as such, company finances are kept separate from the personal finances of its owner(s). There are two types of limited company:

1 **PRIVATE LIMITED COMPANIES** in which there are one or more shareholders. These can be individuals within the company or outsiders, such as business angels, or other companies. The key here is that no shares are offered to the general public. Because shareholders, including the company directors, have invested in the business, they can share in its success through dividends.

2 **PUBLIC LIMITED COMPANIES** in which there must be a minimum of two shareholders and which can offer their shares to the general public. To fall into this category, the company must have issued shares to the value of at least £50,000 before it is able to trade.

Raising finance, if it's required, can come from a small number of sources. As with the sole-trader option, loans can be taken out to get the business going and, in addition, financing can come from shareholders. The advantage here is that the shareholders have an incentive to invest in the business because they have the opportunity to share in its growth. This is the basis of the popular TV programme *Dragon's Den* in which business angels invest in a fledgling business for a share of the company (which in my mind is always way too high for the level of investment required by the entrepreneurs, but I guess it makes good viewing). The final funding mechanism open to the limited company is retained profits, which can be used to fund growth and new projects without the need to take out a loan. Public limited companies have the additional option of raising capital by selling their shares on the stock market.

Although shareholders own the company, they aren't responsible for its management; this is the job of the company director(s). Directors' responsibilities encompassed within the Companies Act 2006 include:

- showing the skill expected of a person with the appropriate knowledge and experience;
- acting as a reasonable person would do looking after their own business;
- treating all shareholders equally;
- declaring any conflicts of interest;
- not making personal profits at the company's expense;
- preparing proper accounts and sending the required documents to Companies House;
- complying with other laws, such as those associated with health and safety, employment law and tax;
- being responsible for the actions of company employees.

If a company director fails to meet some or all of these obligations, he or she may be subject to a fine, disqualification from being a director in the future, personal liability for the company's debts or even a criminal conviction. Of course, as a new company with perhaps just you as the only director, many of the above responsibilities will be less significant in the short term, but you need to be aware of what's required of you. Although this may seem to be too much like hard work, you can always employ a good accountant to reduce some of the real and perceived burden. Using an accountant also gives you peace of mind that you're complying with the most up-to-date rules, regulations and laws associated with running a company.

As the above suggests, there's more paperwork and effort involved with setting up the company than being a sole trader, but most of it is very straightforward and there's plenty of help available if you need it, such as from Companies House or Business Link (see Useful Links at the end of this book). The most important thing you have to do is to register your company with Companies House – a procedure known as 'incorporation'. You'll also need to appoint at least one company director (two if it's a public limited company). You'll also need to appoint a company secretary, if you intend to have a public limited company (since October 2008, private limited companies no longer require company secretaries). The day-to-day management of the business rests with the company directors, which if there's more than one means that some of the control you would have as a sole trader will have been lost. As the company grows, it's likely that you'll have a board of directors who jointly will run the business. This avoids some of the problems that occur when a start-up company outgrows the entrepreneur who established it. Very often entrepreneurs are unwilling to let go of the reins and attempt to control everything, when it's clear that they have neither the time nor skills to do so. If left unchecked, the company can eventually fail, or at the very least never reach its full potential.

The additional complexity which comes with the limited-company option requires more finance-related paperwork. Unlike sole traders who have to submit their annual tax return, the company has to file its accounts with Companies House. The accounts also have to be audited by an accountant so that they represent a true and fair record of the company's financial position. With respect to tax, the company has to make an annual return to HMRC and must pay corporation tax on its profits. The rate at which corporation tax is payable depends on the amount of a company's profits for the financial year in question. Corporation tax is charged at the small companies' rate (currently 21 per cent and rising to 22 per cent in 2009/10) on profits up to £300,000, and the main rate (currently 28 per cent) where profits exceed £1,500,000. The employees of the company must pay NICs and of course tax on their incomes. The company directors are also responsible for notifying Companies House of any changes to the structure or management of the business. Although this sounds like a lot of extra work, it isn't as much as it seems and, once again, employing a good accountant will help considerably.

The biggest benefit in adopting this kind of company structure is the limitation of liability. Unlike the sole trader who's liable for all losses, under the limited-company structure the shareholders aren't liable. Liability lies within the company, not the people. This provides additional comfort to those who feel that the risks are too great if they followed the sole-trader route and often outweighs the additional management and administrative overhead. Shareholders may, of course, lose any money they may have invested into the business, and if they have guaranteed any loans taken out by the business, they'll be liable for these as well.

Partnership

A partnership is more like being a sole trader than working under the umbrella of a limited company. Partnerships need two or more people who are willing to not only work together, but to also share the risks, costs, effort and, of course, the benefits of being in business together. As with a sole trader, in a partnership there's no distinction between the partners and the firm, which means that if the business fails there's no protection from the potential financial losses that might be incurred. All partners are jointly liable for the debts owned by the partnership. It's simple and flexible both to establish and operate and, so long as there are at least two partners, it can continue to operate. Should a partner die, resign or go bankrupt, the partnership will have to be dissolved. Naturally, if there are more than two partners then this wouldn't be the case.

However, going into partnership does require some careful thought and shouldn't be entered into lightly (as is the case with any business arrangement). You have to be comfortable with your fellow partner(s) and it's always a good idea to draw up the basis for the partnership, which would need to include how profits are shared. The simplest way is to share profits equally between all the partners, though many partnerships operate a points system that directly affects the amount of money individual partners earn. For example, in the Big Four accountancies, such as Ernst & Young and PricewaterhouseCoopers, points are awarded for the client-facing roles partners perform and the positions they hold. Other factors also come into play such as sales and delivery, but these tend to impact their share of the profits rather than their core income. Depending on the nature of the partnership, you should consider creating a balanced set of performance measures which can be used to assess contribution and hence the share of the profits which each partner will receive at the end of the financial year.

From a financial perspective, the partnership structure is similar to the sole trader in that:

- each partner is classed as self-employed;
- raising capital involves dipping into personal assets or taking out loans, although it's possible to have sleeping partners who only contribute financially;
- partners have to complete their own self-assessment tax returns each year based on their income and share of the profits.

Partnerships can employ staff and in some cases may engage someone to run the business on their behalf, leaving the partners to perform the duties in which they are expert, such as law for example. As with a limited company, income and expenditure records have to be maintained and the partnership also has to file an annual return to HMRC, but not Companies House in this instance.

I've worked within partnerships for many years and have two observations about them. First, unlike a company structure where people will have defined roles and responsibilities and are in essence working for the greater good of the company, partners are in general working for themselves and as such the question of ownership often arises. I've seen many examples of individual partners refusing to follow a particular course of action or pursuing their own interests to the detriment of the partnership as a whole. So, although the partnership structure offers greater flexibility and fluidity, this can be lost if the working relationships get spoiled by egos. This is why drawing up a partnership agreement is so important. My second observation is that partnerships tend to attract those who want to remain technical specialists rather than management generalists, which tends to be the case in limited companies. It's no surprise that lawyers, accountants and architects tend to opt for partnerships.

Limited-liability partnership

A limited-liability partnership combines the benefits of the partnership structure with that of the limited company. In essence it's both a legal entity and a corporate body, which means that, like a limited company, the legal entity is separate from that of its members. A limited-liability partnership can do all the things a limited company can, including making contracts, holding property and becoming insolvent. However, despite the similarities, the partners within a limited-liability partnership are not employees and are still classed as self-employed. In this case, the individual partners, or limited companies that are integral to it, share in the risks, costs, benefits and running of the business. The emergence of the limited-liability partnership is interesting since one of the most vocal proponents for this type of structure came from the Big Four Accountancies following the demise of Arthur Andersen, the multidisciplinary consulting firm. The firm was prosecuted in 2002 for the obstruction of justice related to its work for Enron. Arthur Andersen took on the role of internal audit within Enron while serving as the external auditor and earning huge fees for its consultancy work. Although this practice should have raised significant conflicts of interest, it was the shredding of Enron documents in the Houston office of Andersen following the Enron's indictment that led to US government decision to indict the company. This resulted in a significant loss of confidence in the firm and the meltdown of Andersen's international network. Andersen ceased to exist and its network was absorbed into the remaining firms (Ernst & Young, PricewaterhouseCoopers, Deloitte and KPMG). The remaining firms claimed that if there was no protection from unlimited liabilities, some or all of the remaining firms could also fail. As a result all have since become limited-liability partnerships.

Setting up a limited-liability partnership is as involved as establishing a limited company and in this case you can't purchase a company name off the shelf. As with a limited company, the limited-liability partnership has to be registered with Companies House (incorporation). Within this structure you have to appoint designated members (similar to the director roles in a limited company). The designated members, of which there should be a minimum of two, have the following responsibilities:

- appointing an auditor (if one is needed);
- signing the accounts on behalf of the members;
- delivering the accounts to the registrar at Companies House;
- notifying the registrar of any membership changes or change to the registered office address or name of the limited-liability partnership;
- preparing, signing and delivering to the registrar an annual return;
- acting on behalf of the limited-liability partnership if it is wound up and dissolved.

As with the pure form of partnerships, it's wise to draw up an agreement between the partners as to how individual performance is to be rewarded. And from a financial perspective, the limited-liability partnership operates in an identical fashion to the pure-partnership structure apart from the requirement to submit an annual return to Companies House.

If you prefer to have the security that comes with limited liability, you may want to consider establishing your company as a limited-liability partnership as opposed to a limited company. The principal advantages of this approach include the following:

- changes to the membership is simple and straightforward and facilitates the expansion of the business by bringing in new partners;
- there's less public scrutiny mainly because the partnership agreement remains confidential to the partners and can't be viewed by the public;
- it's easy to adjust the share allocations between partners, plus there's less administration associated with their issue and allocation.

The only downside with the limited liability structure is that it's still quite new, although most advisers believe it will grow in popularity.

Franchise

Franchises are popular with many freelancers because of the added security they bring. The fundamental advantage of buying into a franchise is that you're getting involved with an established business rather than having to build everything from scratch. When you follow this route, you're buying a licence to use the name, products, services and support systems of the franchiser company. And as you'd suspect, there are plenty of franchise opportunities available including printing and design, automotive, retail, business to business and cleaning companies, to name but a few. The licence you buy normally covers a specific geographical area and runs for a set period of time, after which you can renew (assuming, of course, you've met all of the terms of the franchise agreement). The other advantage this has over the other options is the support the franchiser will typically provide when you start up your business.

From a legal-structure perspective, a franchise can be any one of the preceding structures (sole trader, partnership, limited company). Therefore the nature and form of the franchise will depend on what structure you decide to adopt. This also impacts the financial dimension of the business, although in this case you'll incur additional costs related to the initial fee associated with buying the franchise (which can be significant – the average start-up cost was £64,900 in 2007), the ongoing management fees, the percentage of your profits you'll pay the franchiser and the purchase of the franchiser's products.

Unlike the other structures, there'll be some limitations associated with how the company is run: after all, you'll be part of a broader business with some established rules, processes and procedures. Of course, there may be some flexibility, but ultimately you'll need to recognise that you're buying a business 'out of a box' and you'll have to comply with the way the franchise is operated if you're to be successful. So you should expect to have some additional administrative overhead over and above that associated with the structure you adopt (see previous sections and table below). However, following the franchise route can be an ideal way to break from your existing employer and become more of your own boss – and this is especially appealing to those who are unwilling to make a complete break.

The table below provides a simple summary of the different structures you can adopt so that you compare them at a glance.

Each of the structures covered in this chapter have advantages and disadvantages, and your choice of structure will depend on a range of factors including:

- the level of security you want;
- how much flexibility and freedom you want to run the business;
- the tax position;

- how you want to appear to your clients;
- whether you have other colleagues or potential partners you want to go into business with;
- the ambitions you have for your company.

There may be other additional factors, of course, and because establishing your company is such an important step, remember that it's always best to seek advice from an accountant or similar expert when considering your options.

Aspect	Sole trader	Limited-liability company	Partnership	Limited-liability partnership	Franchise
Management	Self-directed	Shared with fellow directors	Shared with fellow partners	Shared with fellow partners	Defined by the franchiser
Type of employment	Self-employed	Employed	Self-employed	Self-employed	As per structure chosen
Financial backing	Own assets or loan	Own assets, sales of shares, loans and retained profit	Own assets, loans and sleeping partners	Own assets, loans	Own assets or loan (for initial fees associated with buying into the franchise)
Records	Income and expenditure	Standard accounts (profit & loss, cash flow, balance sheet)	Income and expenditure	Standard accounts (profit & loss, cash flow, balance sheet)	Depends on the legal structure chosen; likely to include detailed financial accounts required by the franchiser

Accounts	Annual self-assessment tax return	Annual return to Companies House and HMRC. Accounts have to be audited	Annual self-assessment tax return for each partner and an annual return for the partnership to HMRC	Annual self-assessment tax return for each partner and an annual return for the partnership to HMRC and Companies House. Accounts have to be audited	Depends on the legal structure chosen
Profits	Retained by the sole trader	Retained by the company, distributed through share dividends	Shared across the partners either equally or by some predetermined formula	Shared across the partners either equally or by some predetermined formula	A percentage of the profits will be paid to the franchiser. The remainder will be treated as per the chosen structure

(Continued)

Aspect	Sole trader	Limited-liability company	Partnership	Limited-liability partnership	Franchise
Tax	Profits taxed as income	Profits subject to corporation tax	Profits taxed as income	Profits taxed as income, and corporation tax as appropriate	As per structure chosen
National Insurance Contributions (NICs)	Fixed rate Class 2 NICs and Class 4 on profits	Employee Class 1 NICS	Fixed rate Class 2 NICs and Class 4 on profits	Fixed rate Class 2 NICs and Class 4 on profits	As per structure chosen
Liability	Unlimited	Limited	Unlimited	Limited	As per structure chosen

Finance 101 – Getting the basics right

Finance isn't everyone's forte, but when you work for yourself, it's essential that you put some work into understanding the basics. Without this understanding, it's all too easy to become confused and get into difficulties even if you're running a straightforward operation. So, what finance knowledge should a freelancer have? The profit-and-loss account (P&L) and the balance sheet are musts, as you'll see below.

The profit and loss account (P&L)

The P&L is, in essence, a record of what you've earned and what you've spent in order to run your business. In other words, it's a record of what money comes into and goes out of your company over a given period, be it a month, quarter or year. The difference between the two is the profit (or loss) from your business activities – a very important thing to know.

The P&L seeks to demonstrate how much has been made or lost over that given period, starting with the value of sales – excluding the value of VAT charged, if registered (see later on in this chapter why it's a good idea to register for

VAT) minus the total expenditure of all categories (salaries, rent, rates, stationery, travel, supplies and so on) – excluding VAT again, if registered. Remember, if you *are* registered for VAT, you must account for your VAT to HMRC on the quarterly VAT return (more on this in Chapter 8). Subject to the complication of VAT, this part is quite straightforward – income less expenditure.

To help understand what the P&L shows, see opposite for a very simple example for a company that sells both goods and services (note this is for illustrative purposes only).

As you can see, the P&L is arranged vertically with income at the top (which, in the case of the example opposite, is sales). Below this are grouped together certain costs that comprise the costs associated with trading (that is, the cost of goods and/or services sold). These may include direct labour costs (these are the costs associated with employing people in your firm, such as a secretary for example), goods or materials consumed in support of sales and other 'direct' costs. Subtracting the cost of goods sold from your income gives the gross profit. Depending on the nature of your freelance business, the cost of goods sold will vary, but in many cases it will be the cost of selling your services. Gross profit, an important indicator of business trading performance, should be tracked and compared regularly – every month is best.

Profit and Loss Account for Year ended December 31, 2007

			£000
Sales			816
Less:	Opening stock	36	
	Purchases	352	
	Less closing stock	−42	
	Cost of Goods Sold		346
	Direct Labour		106
			452
	Gross Profit		364
Less:	Other salaries, NI and pension	190	
	Rent, rates	35	
	Power	6	
	Travel, entertainment	15	
	Insurance	2	
	Stationery, post, IT consumables	4	
	Depreciation	12	
	Increase in bad debt provision	5	
	Repairs, maintenance	7	
	Marketing, advertising	5	
			281
	Earning before interest and tax (EBIT)		83
	Interest earned		2
	Net profit before tax		85
	Provision for taxation		50
	Net Profit for year		35

Below the gross profit number are listed other items of expenditure of an indirect nature. Typically, this includes items such as administration costs, travel, depreciation (if you have equipment, such as computers, faxes and photocopiers for example), building costs and so on. The total of all these items is then deducted from the gross profit to produce the net profit. You then need to take into account tax and any interest you may have earned from cash in the bank over the course of the period you are looking at. Finally, you get to see your 'bottom line'. This is the profit you've earned for the year after tax has been deducted. This figure is what you're really interested in, as it's linked to your earnings, dividend payments if you make them and any bonuses you might distribute. It's also the number that links the P&L to the balance sheet, explained below.

The balance sheet

The balance sheet is also important because it shows what a company owns and what it is owed. In essence, it's a snapshot of the net worth of the business. While the P&L shows the flow of money in and out of the business over time, the balance sheet shows you the state of play *on a given date* and is similar to the opening or closing balance on the statements you receive from your bank. Very simply, the balance sheet lists all the money owned or owed to the business (the assets) and all the money owed by the business (the liabilities). To help understand what the balance sheet reveals, here is a very simple example (note

---

Balance Sheet as at December 31, 2007

			£000
Ordinary Shares, authorised, issued and fully paid			50
Profits carried forward from prior years			71
Profit for the year			35
			156
Represented by:			

Fixed Assets	Cost	Depn.	WDV	
Motor Vehicles	81	25	56	
IT equipment	31	9	22	
	112	34	78	78

Current Assets		
Cash at Bank and in hand	75	
Debtors less provision	39	
Stock	42	
		156

Less: Current Liabilities		
Creditors	17	
NI, PAYE	11	
Corporation Tax	50	
		78
Working Capital		78
		156

---

that Depn is shorthand for depreciation and WDV is the written down value of your assets after depreciation).

As you can see, the balance sheet has three sections:

1   shareholders' equity
2   assets
3   liabilities

The first section (shareholder's equity) includes the value of shares if you have issued any; long-term loans to the organisation if you have any; any reserves (money you've retained from your previous years' trading) plus or minus the cumulative profit or loss (remember the net profit or bottom line number from the P&L). It's usual to say that this amount is represented by (or equal to) the net assets which are set out in the next section.

The second section (assets) includes cash and bank deposits; the value of any inventory you hold which includes raw materials, buildings if you own them, part-completed work in progress and any finished items (your stock); money which is owed to you by your clients (your debtors as they are known in the UK); any pre-payments you may have made (for example the money you pay in advance for rent and phones) and any fixed assets (which includes plant, machinery, office equipment and computers). Because assets depreciate over their useful life (see above), you need to take this into account when arriving at your net asset figure. For example, in the case of a computer, each year one third of the original cost will be 'charged' to the P&L with the balance sheet showing the written down value (WDV) of the computer and all other assets. When an asset is sold or scrapped, any remaining value will be charged to the P&L. Equally, if an asset is sold at a profit or above its WDV, the additional amount is included in the P&L.

The final section (liabilities) includes the money you owe to your suppliers; any short-term loans you might have from the bank; any long-term loans you might have, although few freelancers tend to have these as they're normally the preserve of the bigger companies who need to raise capital on the financial markets, and any provisions against bad debt you might need to make (clients who don't pay).

Your net current asset value is therefore derived from subtracting your current liabilities from your current assets. Ideally net current assets should be positive with current assets exceeding current liabilities as this is a strong indication of the ability to trade, which is very important. This difference is also known as working capital and measures how much in liquid assets a company has available to build its business. As mentioned above, ideally this number should be positive, although it can be negative and depends on how much debt the company is carrying. In general, companies that have a lot of working capital will be more successful since they can expand and improve their operations (something to bear in mind if you want to grow your business over time). Companies with negative working capital may lack the funds necessary for growth.

In summary then, a company's net assets are the fixed assets added to the net current assets and are equal to the capital section. This being the case the balance sheet is by definition, in balance.

Other finance-related issues

Maintaining a set of accounts will go a long way to helping you stay on top of your business's financial position and will establish some vitally important financial disciplines. However, there are a few other things you also need to consider: the sections below should be a good starting point.

Minimising your outgoings

All businesses, whatever their size, should be aiming to increase their income as well as cut down on their spending.

■ **REGISTER FOR VAT.** Strictly speaking, you only need to register for VAT when the turnover (income) of your business exceeds the limit defined by HMRC. This turnover figure changes most years and as of April 2008 it was £67,000. However, even if you're turning over less than this you might want to consider registering as you'll be able to reclaim the VAT you've paid on certain purchases, so long as you retain the invoice which should contain the supplier's VAT registration number. There are exceptions and you need to follow the rules set out by HMRC. For example, meals and entertaining are excluded, but it's a good idea to keep up to date using the HMRC website or asking your accountant as the rules do change from time to time. You must pay that additional VAT to HMRC every quarter summarised on the VAT return. Another upside of being registered is that you have the temporary cash-flow advantage of charging VAT – but remember to have the funds available ready to pay at the end of the quarter.

- If your spouse or partner becomes a director of the company, you can take advantage of all or any unused part of their **personal tax allowance if they're on the payroll** – a definite advantage. But see Chapter 8, as HMRC changes the tax rules continuously and you don't want to fall foul of these since being faced with an investigation can be both time-consuming, potentially costly and above all worrying (more on this in Chapter 8).

- **DEPRECIATE YOUR ASSETS.** Defined simply, depreciation is the decrease in the value of an object over time. As the equipment you use as a freelancer depreciates, it becomes worn or outdated and as repairs to it become difficult and expensive you'll want to replace it. So instead of writing-off the entire value of a large purchase (such as a

£2,100 laptop computer, for example) in the year of acquisition, it's good practice to spread the cost over the asset's useful life (in this case your computer). So in the case of your £2,100 you would write it off over a three-year period, or £700 per year. In such instances, the annual depreciation charges go to the P&L and the WDV remains on the balance sheet (as shown on both financial statements above).

- Dividend payments, made against the previous year's profits, can be received without need to pay employers' National Insurance (relevant if you've set your business up as a limited company). This approach to paying yourself is very popular with freelancers because it reduces their overall tax liability. However, HMRC takes a dim view of people who only pay themselves by dividends – there must be evidence of employers' National Insurance paid through a pay as you earn (PAYE) scheme.

General good practice

There's plenty of advice available which discusses the value of following good practice when it comes to financial management. Indeed, this is why accounting regulations exist. You'll be pleased to hear that I won't be covering these here, and will instead focus on some more general areas of good practice, all of which are easy to implement.

- Always keep your receipts, invoices and if appropriate, business mileage log.

- If you do need to reclaim mileage (which many freelancers do), use HMRC published rates rather than having a company car and paying punitive levels of tax.

- Keep your private and business banking arrangements separate – it will avoid any confusion. This can be useful when you may need to raise finance and besides, no institution should have too much information about you – privacy is increasingly important.

- Find a good accountant who can give up-to-date tax advice and produce monthly accounts if you don't have the time, knowledge or confidence to do it yourself. You'd be better off concentrating on developing your business than trying to keep current on tax issues. If at all possible, ask a trusted friend or associate if they can recommend someone.

- If you decide to have a limited company, then it's wise to run a proper PAYE scheme, pay a monthly salary and keep up to date with your income tax and NICs. Remember that you'll now pay both employers and employees NICs once it's your business.

- Pay your corporation and all other taxes on time otherwise fines apply. Your accountant will calculate your liability for you and advise you when to pay.

- A very important rule: surplus cash is not profit! I repeat, surplus cash does not equal profit. It is, however, an indication that either you have good cash flow and/or you haven't paid some bills.

- Don't assume that you have to buy everything you need for your business – you could rent if you don't have the cash available. It's the use of an asset that's important, not its ownership. However, if you've the cash available, it's often better to buy than lease simply because borrowing other people's money is always more expensive than using your own.

- Study your accounts every month. Look out for areas where your spend is accelerating. If it's supporting higher levels of sales and you're getting a good return, then that's fine. If not, you need to cut back. And cut back quickly!

- Set financial goals as well as business goals and review them regularly.

Invoicing and paying your bills

The perennially thorny issue of how to get paid on time is always tricky (see Chapter 6 for more detailed advice), but for now here are a few key points to remember about invoicing and paying your bills.

- Don't presume that because you're making money today, you will be tomorrow. A sale is only complete when you've been paid for the work done or the goods sold, and even then, customers can sometimes ask for their money back. So it's a very good idea to keep some cash reserves in the bank just in case.

- Pay your bills when they're due. Late payments can put your suppliers' noses out of joint and make them reluctant to work with you again. And you'll only benefit financially for one month anyway. Remember that some of your suppliers may be self-employed too and would you wish to be treated like that?

- When you start your business, unless you expect to produce numerous invoices each day (for example, in a low-value/high-volume business, such as preparing personal tax returns) don't number your invoices with a sequence that begins with '1' as it makes you look very new. It's all about perception management. So long as you keep a summary of all invoices raised (in an invoice register) and copies of those invoices which are kept in the same order as issued, the number on the invoice is unimportant. For example, consider starting with 3051 one month and next month start with 3268; it really doesn't matter and your accountant won't mind so long as your invoices can be uniquely identified. You could also consider even alpha-numeric invoice numbers, for example invoice no: AC1001.

So there you have it, finance 101. There is, of course, much more to finance than there's room for here, but the important thing is that we've addressed the basics. At the very least, you can consider the most important aspects and will hopefully feel a little more comfortable with some of the accounting terms and when speaking to your accountant. And ever: always seek professional advice if you're unsure about anything.

Ultimately, running a business means that you have to be financially literate and be able to gauge the financial health of your company. You don't have to become a qualified accountant to do so, but it's worth studying a few books so that you're familiar with the common terms and processes and it's worth taking some basic courses too – the investment is well worth it.

Maximising your income

Whatever your motivations for moving into freelance work, the one thing you need to ensure is that you're getting the value that you deserve. This may sound obvious but many freelancers don't give this sufficient thought before they sign their first contract. The key thing to remember is that you have quite a bit of control over what you get paid and hence the income line on the profit-and-loss statement introduced in Chapter 3. And let's face it, when it comes to financial issues for freelancers, how much you charge should be right at the top of the list.

What price your expertise?

For you to maximise your income, you need to understand the value of what you bring to your clients. Once you know this, you can work out the price to charge or at least be ready to negotiate when the need arises. Assessing your skills as described above is a very good start, but there's quite a bit more you can do.

In general, freelancers determine their fees by considering a range of things, such as their level of expertise and knowledge, the market for their skills and the expenses they need to cover (as discussed in Chapter 1). Of these, it's the market that you'll need to consider quite carefully and this is where some research comes in handy. Understanding what the market will bear can be helpful in establishing your rates, so finding out what fellow freelancers get paid can be useful, as can contacting agencies or trade bodies who usually undertake annual surveys to assess market rates. These often indicate the rates by different market sectors (publishing, fast-moving consumer goods and so on), but remember that if the competition is stiff, the prices are likely to be lower than you may have hoped for and lower than indicated in the surveys. However, surveys are helpful because they'll show you the maximum and minimum rates which are currently achievable and hence give you a sense of whether your ideal fee is within the right ball park.

Ultimately, though, your services must be priced so that you make a profit and to do this you should think seriously about the following:

- How does your rate compare to what others are charging? Is it higher or lower? What does that tell you about the market?
- How important is the assignment to your potential client? Is it highly valuable and therefore less price sensitive, or vice versa? It's certainly

worth asking: you may be surprised at the answer and it's a great way to manage expectations.

- How *significant* is the client's problem? This question is slightly different to the one above, as it's focused on the nature of the problem, rather than the value of the solution. The two go hand in hand, of course, but it's often too easy to focus on the solution without spending enough time understanding the problem. Make sure you spend enough time fully exploring and defining the problem: it may be bigger or more complex than you first thought.

- How quickly does the assignment have to be completed? If there's a tight deadline, it's often possible to charge a premium for finishing your work quickly. 'Rush jobs' can also demonstrate your flexibility and reliability and may well lead to a long-term relationship.

- What does your price say about you and your services? In some cases, it's better to price high and be willing to walk away (more on this below). If you pitch too low price-wise, it may look as if you're desperate for work or you're falling into the trap of winning work by bidding low (which happens a lot). There's a fine balance to be struck here and it's not always easy, especially if there's been a gap between assignments for a client.

Also, don't forget all you've learnt in your career thus far, as this may help you to establish a higher price for your expertise. If you've worked for a variety of major employers over the years before you moved into a freelance role, you'll have gained some valuable experience and training and developed some great skills. Don't ignore these, especially if you're pitching for a specialist assignment.

Creative ways to maximise your profit

Your aim as a freelancer is to maximise your income, and knowing the value you bring is an essential component to achieving this. It's inevitable, though, that you'll come up against situations where the client will try to keep the price down. So how can you deal with this? Working from the premise that you should be aiming to make somewhere between 15 and 30 per cent profit, with an average of 20 per cent, there are a few things you could do to ensure that you hold your rates up, including:

- **BEING PREPARED TO WALK AWAY.** As mentioned above, there'll be some occasions where it's better to walk away from an offer of work than to set the precedent of accepting lower rates. As soon as you accept a lower rate, your clients will use that as a benchmark and want to pay you at a lower level from that point on. If you're prepared to walk away, you could be surprised by the reaction to this, especially when the client values what you bring to them. This happened to one of my fellow partners recently, when she was asked to drop her daily rate. The rate was too low given the value that she had established for her work, and she decided to tell them that she was unwilling to renew the contract. As the contract came very close to its agreed end date, the client came back and agreed to pay her the usual rate. And although she'd mentally prepared to leave the client, she renewed. So the lesson here is to know your value, set your price and be willing to walk away if the client is unwilling to meet it.

■ **HAVING DIFFERENT RATES FOR DIFFERENT KINDS OF ASSIGNMENTS.** As mentioned above, it's important to have different pricing structures in place to cover rush jobs or particularly specialised assignments. You should also define the ranges in which you'll work as well as the ideal target. If the agreed price is within the range, great; if it's below you might opt to walk away, and if it's more, then that means you'll make more profit.

■ **CONSIDERING BONUS PAYMENTS OR OTHER OUTCOME-DRIVEN INCENTIVES.** Some clients, for instance, may be willing to offer a bonus at the end of a contract in exchange for a lower hourly rate. This is something I often do, as it helps in the negotiations and means you can end up with a lump sum at the end of the contract (which can be very handy, especially if it will be a while before you seek out your next assignment). If you do this, be careful to agree the basis for the performance bonus upfront and make sure the basis for payment is transparent and easily assessed.

■ **STARTING OFF AT A RELATIVELY LOW RATE, BUT AGREEING TO AN INCREASE AT A SET POINT IN TIME (OR WHEN THE**

CONTRACT IS RENEWED). This is also quite common and a good way to start work with a client who may have a limited budget to begin with. In this scenario, it's essential to keep your standard rate in mind and to agree the best time with the client to increase the (temporarily) lower rate that you've taken on. You may find that once a client starts to work with you and begins to depend on your input and expertise, this is quite an easy process.

- **AVOIDING GIVING YOUR TIME AWAY FOR FREE, TEMPTING THOUGH IT IS.** Most freelancers do the odd thing here and there for their clients which eventually mount up and represent quite a lot of time and lost income. Be quite clear on the number of hours you're going to work and agree a ceiling with the client. You may also agree an overtime rate if you're working out of standard hours. The only exception you should make is when your client is asking for a discount. As mentioned in relation to walking away from a job, discounting merely lowers the price expectation in the future and eats away at your margin. A better approach is to keep the rate the same but throw in a small number of free days. In this way you avoid eroding your margins.

- **'VALUE BILLING' YOUR CLIENT.** This is a tricky one and one which many of the professions, such as law, accountancy and consultancy have been struggling with for years. In an environment which is used to being paid by the hour or by the day, the concept of value billing is a hard one to grasp. But if you can crack it, it's well worth it. What you *won't* be doing is charging by the hour or day, but instead will offer your client a single price. Remember that although there might be other people out there who could do a similar job, you might be able to complete it to a much higher quality and also much faster. If that's the case, you should factor this into your fee for the work, otherwise all you'll end up doing is costing the client less for better work – and that doesn't seem right.

When it comes to maximising your income, there's nothing like preparation. So the next time you're getting ready for your next client meeting consider what skills, expertise and experience you bring; understand your price points; know your market; prepare your negotiation approach (performance bonuses, being prepared to walk away and so on), but most importantly know your value and stick to it. And remember that it takes time to establish your true value: building a solid reputation is critical to your future, which in turn is predicated on credibility and a good track record of successful assignments. If you get this right, things like value billing will be so much easier.

Having established your value, the next thing to do is to figure out how to source your income, which is the focus of the next chapter – and having a good reputation is not a bad way to start.

5 Sourcing your work

The good news about freelance work is that you can sell your skills to a wider audience than you could if you stayed in full-time employment. Having spent years working for a range of employers, both large and small, the fundamental problem I recognised is that you can only sell your skills and capabilities to a small audience. Now if this audience is unable, or perhaps unwilling, to use the many skills, capabilities and expertise you possess, it won't be too long before frustration sets in. The same issue applies when you want to progress up the career ladder: this tends to be based upon a narrow set of skills defined by other people, and – generally speaking – if you don't match it, you won't get promoted. It's important to recognise that you have many more options open to you as a freelancer, some of which are mentioned in Chapter 1.

The biggest downside, of course, is that you have to be willing to sell yourself much more often which can be difficult. Let's face it, few of us are natural salespeople. But you can see from the last chapter that your ability to justify your price and negotiate the deal you want will depend largely on your ability to sell. And, irrespective of how you source your work, there'll be some salesmanship required. So before looking at the ways in which you can find work as a freelancer, it's worth making a brief departure into the art of selling.

Life's a pitch

I read a great book some time ago called *Life's a Pitch* (Stephen Bayley and Roger Mavity, Bantam, 2007) which, as you'd expect, is all about the art of selling. One of the reasons I liked it more than other books on the same theme was that it this takes a deeper look at why selling yourself is such a crucial skill. It's also an easy read and very insightful on all sales-related matters ('pitching', as the authors call it), whether it be at interview, over lunch or in a formal setting such as a presentation. I'll leave you to pick up the book if you want to, but even if you are doing little in the way of pitching, there are a few nuggets to be aware of, including:

■ although you might think that logic and information are key when selling your services, it's often your emotions that clinch the deal and by the same token it's delivery that matters more than content. This is not to say you can ignore content, but rather you need to think carefully about how it's delivered.

- when pitching into a client, agency or even someone who's part of your own network, you need to make sure your presentation addresses both the problem and the solution. Although this is obvious, we all have a tendency to go straight to solution mode when presented with a problem to solve. However, focusing too much on providing information about the solution prevents the audience you are selling to from connecting with you on the problem (after all that's why you are talking to them in the first place). Empathise with them about their problem and you'll gain their trust when it comes to how their problem can be resolved.

- confidence is vital, as without this you'll find it difficult to secure any work as a freelancer. Remember, one of the attributes of a successful freelancer is a strong sense of self-worth.

- first impressions count. We've been told this many times, but so many of us fail to listen to the message. It's very important to consider how you want to be perceived by those you're pitching to, as this can make a real difference to the outcome.

I guess the point to all this is that as a freelancer, you face a paradox. On the one hand, you've endless possibilities and opportunities to sell yourself and your expertise, while on the other you have to work at it to beat the competition, which at times will be pretty stiff. Central to success, therefore, is adopting a professional attitude to sales irrespective of how you source your work.

Finding and generating your work

How you find work will depend very much on the level of effort you put into it and how much control you want to have over your income. At one extreme, there are the agencies who will 'sell' you to their clients and at the other, there's business development where it's more likely that you'll be making sales pitches yourself. As you've probably guessed, in the former you have less control over your income, while in the latter you've more. There are six principal means of sourcing work:

1   using agencies
2   networking
3   becoming an associate of other firms
4   reputation and referrals
5   Internet marketing
6   cold calling and sales pitches

Using agencies

Agencies are certainly one of the easiest ways to source work, as they do the graft for you. They work on the simple premise of selling in freelance help to their clients with whom they have relationships (some of which are exclusive). They make their money by charging their clients one fee and paying you another (lower, of course). For example, they may charge you out to their client at £50 per hour but pay you £40, which is fine if you're willing to go with the rate they offer. With the explosion of interest in freelance work, the number of agencies has increased dramatically – and these days it's possible to find an agency promoting both niche and general roles. In fact, they pretty much cater for almost every type of freelance work you can think of, from copywriting right through to Web design.

Agencies are quite a bit different from what they used to be, with the human touch having been largely replaced by sophisticated search technologies, and this has implications for you and how you approach and work with them. Most maintain databases of freelancers which they search every time a new role comes in from one of their clients. Searches are typically made against key words contained in the freelancer's CV or profile (such as 'project manager' or 'software tester') and when there's a match, you tend to get a call. At the same time, you're free to search for roles on their websites and apply for those you find interesting. If you're put forward for a position, you usually have a discussion with the agent, followed by an interview with the client.

The upsides to using agencies include:

- they have access to a large number of potential clients and assignments which would be impossible to maintain yourself;
- the work will come to you rather than you having to look for it yourself;
- they take out 99 per cent of the effort needed to secure a role, leaving you to wow the client;
- they administer the payment of fees from their clients, which removes the major headache of bill chasing from you;
- they sometimes offer incentives and bonus payments;
- they can put you forward for multiple roles at the same time, which hedges your bets should any fall through;
- some agencies now offer benefits such as networking and resources to help you develop.

However, there are also a few downsides to using agencies:

- they increasingly treat those on their databases as commodities rather than individuals, using little more than keyword searches to select potential candidates;
- you can be inundated with roles that aren't suitable – some agencies send out all their roles to everyone on their database irrespective of whether they're suitable;
- competition between agencies tends to drive down rates and over time you may find that there's little which meets your income expectations;
- they'll rarely pay you what you're truly worth, because if they did, they'd have little or no profit left;

■ they don't always have your best interests at heart and rarely get to know you; remember that you're a commodity they're trading on the open market – not quite the same as pork bellies, but sometimes not far off!

To get the most out of the agency route, clearly it's best to find those that are most suited to you and your line of work. So the first thing to do is to find the agencies which promote freelancers with similar skills to your own. When carrying out this research, you should tap into any freelancers you might know as they can usually point you in the direction of the better ones and tell you which to avoid. The next thing to do is to register with a small number of them (the better ones, of course). This will extend your coverage, remembering that not all agencies work with the same clients. It also means that you should be getting multiple calls, which is always encouraging, and provides you with more choice, allowing you to select the work you most like and ideally the best rate. Whether we like it or not, there's a greater emphasis than ever on the use of sophisticated search engines, so be sure to keep your profile up to date and check that it includes the key words they'll use to select potential candidates in your area of specialism. It would be worth asking the agency what key words they use before you submit a profile to them, as this will improve your hit rate. Finally, do your best to get to know your agent, as this is likely to pay dividends.

Networking

Social and business networking is now incredibly popular, as the success of sites such as MySpace, Facebook and LinkedIn demonstrates. As a freelancer, networking can be highly valuable because it allows you to:

- promote your skills and capabilities to a wider audience;
- make contact with potential clients;
- find potential business associates;
- seek support and advice when you need it.

Networking opportunities take on many different forms, including:

- face-to-face meetings designed to bring freelancers together to discuss the issues they have, or to provide the opportunity for potential clients and freelancers to meet;
- industry forums where the specific topics of an industry of business sector are debated;
- conferences, seminars and trade shows;
- electronic forums;

- online forums and networking sites where you can connect with other likeminded people.

Before you decide to join a network, think quite carefully about what you hope to get out of it – and, of course, what you're willing to put in. Successful networking requires a degree of reciprocal obligation – you scratch my back, and I'll scratch yours, in short – so if you're not willing to put much into it, your results will be quite meagre. The biggest problem I often come across with networking is that a lot of effort and time can be spent for little return, as although it might be fairly easy to build a large number of contacts, it's surprisingly difficult to maintain a broad network once it's been built. You may also find that a lot of the traffic is one way, with people coming to you for help and free advice, rather than the other way around. If you're not careful, a significant amount of effort and precious time can be wasted.

The other form of networking is with your clients once you've established them. Some people call this 'relationship development', and consider it to be one of the most effective means of securing work. I've a different view, which I explore in reputation and referrals (below). That said, maintaining links with long-standing clients is very important and can be a great way to develop new opportunities. Like most people, your clients tend to move on and will often ask you to work for them in their new role, especially if you did a super job for them first time around. When maintaining contact with them, you have to strike a balance between almost ignoring them, or continuously pestering them. It is a fine line and everyone reacts differently. As a rule, contacting those in your client network every six months is usually sufficient. Of course, if they value what you can do for them, you may find that they contact you, which is even better.

I approach networking in a more limited but targeted way. I have perhaps 20 to 30 people in my network with whom I maintain regular contact. This might involve catching up over a beer one evening, swapping ideas online, a quick phone call to see how things are, working on joint pitches or figuring out how to approach a new client. Focusing my networking around specific topics, academic interests, ideas and clients also helps to ensure that the links remain strong. I don't source much work through my network either, as I tend to keep my client and non-client networks quite separate because each serves a different function. The key thing is to be aware of the potential benefits of networking but also of the realities of it, and not to get so hung up on it that you don't look for work via other routes.

Becoming an associate of other firms

Another useful source of work is through associations with other companies and freelancers, although this is likely to vary according to the type of freelance work you undertake. The shift to freelance work and self-employment in general has meant that most organisations, both large and small, are happy to have both full-time employees and associates on their books. Using associates provides companies with some distinct advantages:

- it allows them to be flexible with the resourcing so that if a large job comes in they can tap into their associate base without impacting their fixed costs;
- it gives them a much larger footprint and hence allows them to appear much larger than perhaps they are (more relevant to small companies);
- it provides them with the opportunity to use specialist skills which are difficult to retain or justify as and when the need arises, which in turn helps them meet the broader demands of their clients.

Developing associate relationships requires quite a bit of effort in that you'll need to do your research and approach firms who might be interested in your skills. This is best treated like a job interview, although in this case your aim is to become part of their associate base rather than a full-time employee. Like agencies, some companies can offer incentives and bonus payments when you work with them.

In my experience, most organisations are receptive to discussions about becoming an associate so it's always worth giving it a try: you have very little to lose in doing so, but plenty to gain. And you may find that over time, as you build your reputation, other companies approach to you to see if you'll join them. For example, some firms use both individual associates who have skills and expertise that are valuable to them and their clients, as well as associate firms who have complementary skills and expertise that they're unlikely to develop. This, in particular, offers some major advantages, not least when approaching larger clients.

The only downside, if indeed there is one, is that in the same way agencies restrict your income by taking a percentage of your gross earnings, becoming an associate means that you have some but not necessarily huge amounts of opportunity to maximise your fees. The rate you'll receive will depend on a range of factors, including the type of work you do, the type of assignments the company wins, profitability, overall fees and so on. Like an agency, the company has to make its margin, but that said, you can often secure better rates by following this route.

Reputation and referrals

Managing your reputation as a freelancer should be your number one priority, for the simple reason that a good reputation will lead to more work through referrals and plenty of repeat work. Once you prove that you're dependable, it'll become easier to secure work. For example, when I moved into a freelance role my first contract came from a company I'd worked with while at PricewaterhouseCoopers. I'd delivered a major systems project for them, and when it came to providing input on an even larger one, they contacted me because I'd helped them before. The same is true of Web developer friends of mine, as well copy editors, proofreaders and indexers in the publishing trade, and software developers in the IT industry.

So what should you do to build and maintain your reputation? Well, some of this should be pretty obvious. A significant amount of your reputation will be based on your ability to deliver well and how dependable you are, as well as your skills, capabilities and expertise. Having developed a solid reputation, you should also seek to make the most of it with your satisfied clients by asking them to refer you to other potential clients. If, for example, you have the head of IT or the head of marketing extolling your virtues to people within his or her network, it will make the job of sourcing work that little bit easier. Better still, you should aim to have your existing client put you in touch with other potential clients. Even if this doesn't generate work immediately, it begins to widen your market presence, which is always a good thing because it helps to build your brand.

Web marketing

Although this may not be on the top of your agenda as a freelancer, there is an expectation today that every business has a website. Irrespective of how many 'hits' your site will get, it's worth having some kind of Web presence because it puts you and your company out there.

If you treat your website as a window on the world, it can be an effective marketing tool with which to communicate what you do to a wider audience. And to make the most of your Web-based marketing, consider the following points:

- **MAKE SURE YOU'RE CLEAR ON THE OBJECTIVES OF YOUR SITE.** For example, you might just want it to provide some basic information about your company and its offerings, or you might want to provide a lot more such as endorsements, case studies, examples of what you do and so on. Spend some time thinking about this as good websites can add to your brand and market presence.

- **THINK CAREFULLY ABOUT YOUR TARGET AUDIENCE.** Will it be your existing clients or the casual viewer? Or both? Depending on the type of work you do, it may be even be worth having a special client area that's password controlled and gives them access to additional material not available elsewhere.

- **MAKE SURE YOU MAXIMISE YOUR HITS WITH THE MAJOR SEARCH ENGINES SUCH AS GOOGLE AND YAHOO.** This process is called 'search engine optimisation'. If your website falls into the top 10 results for a search, you're doing very well and are more likely to get more hits. There are a few things to consider, such as regularly refreshing your content, having plenty of reciprocal links to other websites and offering free content. Although you could do this yourself, it's best to employ a qualified Web designer who'll know all the tricks you can employ and who'll undoubtedly be freelance too!

- **MAKE SURE YOU HAVE THE RIGHT KEYWORDS IN THE TEXT DISPLAYED ON YOUR WEBSITE.** This will mean that any search is able to pick up your site easily.

- **BUILD RECIPROCAL LINKS WITH OTHER WEBSITES.** This is a very good idea if you happen to have associate relationships with other freelancers and companies.

- **CONSIDER INCLUDING A DISCUSSION FORUM** to allow a two-way flow of information and ideas. You'll need to consider who moderates it, although many freelancers do it themselves.

- **KEEP YOUR SITE SIMPLE** so that clients and those who access it find it easy to navigate.

- **KEEP YOUR SITE UP TO DATE** and its content fresh.

Cold calling and pitches

The final approach to winning work is the old-fashioned way: cold calling clients, holding sales meetings, creating proposals, making pitches and negotiating deals. This, as you would suspect, can be time-consuming, frustrating and nerve-wracking. But there's nothing like the feeling of having won some work from all that hard effort you've put into it. I've spent the last 12 years doing this and it does get easier the more you do it, but the sales process is never clear-cut and you rarely win everything you pitch for – but that's the nature of competition.

Below is a summary of the various routes to securing work as a freelancer. In each case, I've indicated the level of influence you have over your income and the amount of effort that's required to make best use of it. As you can see, it varies quite considerably and ultimately, sourcing your work is best achieved by using a combination of the approaches discussed above. The relative emphasis on each is likely to change as you build your reputation: early on, you're more likely to use agencies, but as you gain more experience and contacts, it's more likely that you'll depend on your own capabilities and reputation in the market. The important thing is to consider all channels and use each appropriately.

Building and maintaining a portfolio

One of the topics on which the popular management thinker Charles Handy wrote in his book *The Empty Raincoat* (Hutchinson, 1994) was what he termed the 'portfolio career'. Unlike the typical career path that many of us are familiar with, the portfolio career is geared towards pursuing a mix of employment opportunities simultaneously. As freelancers, we should all be aiming to build a portfolio of clients and work that's large enough to enable us to work on those things that we find interesting and become less driven by the immediate need to put food on the table. The beauty of the portfolio model is that it

Source	Influence over income	Level of effort required
Agencies	Low	Low
Networking	Medium	Medium to High
Associate	Low to Medium	Medium
Reputation and referrals	Medium to High	Low to Medium
Web marketing	Medium	Low
Cold calling and pitches	Medium to High	High

allows freelancers to mix the work they need to do with that which they want to do, and this not only keeps life interesting but allows them to develop new capabilities and satisfy their curiosity.

So far we've covered the financial considerations of leaving the security of full-time employment, setting up your company structure, getting your basic financial disciplines in place, securing the value you deserve and sourcing your work. Of course, there's a little more to finance than this, as there are three additional aspects to consider which are less fun. These are making sure you get paid, avoiding some of the financial pitfalls associated with freelance work and the wonderful topic of tax. So although the next three chapters may not be exciting, they are vital for your financial health.

Getting paid . . . on time

You've put in time and effort to set up your business, win valuable clients and deliver exceptional work. So far, so good. Now you need to make sure that you get paid, which is the whole point of selling your services in the first place. On the face of it, this would seem to be the most straightforward part of what you do, but it can be a real headache. And although many of the problems associated with getting paid are down to the way clients treat their suppliers (especially the bigger ones, unfortunately), there's plenty you can do to get your payment in on time. Being paid in a timely manner is fundamental to managing your cash flow, so it's well worth spending time and effort on this; otherwise, you may find that chasing your clients for unpaid bills consumes too much of your valuable time. Before moving on to what you should be doing to ensure that you get paid on time, let's get two pieces of bad news out of the way.

The first concerns the time it takes UK businesses to pay their bills, which is unfortunately increasing, rather than decreasing. Even over one year – 2006–2007 – the time it took to pay bills increased by two days and is now at an all-time high. According to Experian, which provides information, analytical and marketing services to organisations and the general public, companies are taking an average of 61 days to pay their bills – over two months. What's even worse is that larger companies take on average nearly 82 days to pay. Small and medium-sized companies are a bit better, but are still taking a long time to pay coming in at around the 61 days[1].

According to Experian, the slowest-paying industry is the electricity industry at 72 days, while agriculture is the fastest at 54 days. And according to the Bankers Automated Clearing Services, the value of payments made later than the agreed period rose to £2.6 billion in January 2008 alone. Over the year 2007–2008, the total later-payment burden shouldered by small businesses increased to £18.6 billion – all in all, quite appalling. Of course, these are average numbers, but they give you a sense of what you may be up against and in my mind suggest that you have to be on top of billing even more than perhaps anything else you do as a freelancer.

The second piece of bad news is to do with the general attitudes towards record-keeping and invoicing. Many people are poor at doing these straightforward tasks

[1] See www.bytestart.co.uk

efficiently. For example, some people actually put off invoicing their clients, dismissing it as dull paperwork. The longer it takes to raise an invoice, however, the longer it will take to get paid which, as we've seen above, is not good at the best of times. Next on the list comes poor record-keeping. Failing to keep receipts and recording your time properly tends to compound the time it takes to produce an invoice, as does failing to maintain an effective filing system which keeps everything together. The last thing on my list of bugbears is inaccurate billing. When invoices are sent out with inaccuracies, it may take a while before a dispute is raised. Then you have to recheck the contents of the invoice and may end up reissuing it, losing even more time. To avoid this, make sure that the invoice is clear, addressed to the correct person, has the right reference on it, and includes your VAT number, if appropriate, and payment terms. And check it through a couple of times before sending it out; do everything in your power to speed the process along.

To some extent, the whole business of getting paid is a bit like a game of cat and mouse: even if you're the best record-keeper in the world and always invoice in good time, your client may be under pressure to hold on to their cash for as long as possible. This may have less of an impact on the large companies, but it can be catastrophic for small businesses and freelancers, in particular. Sometimes drastic action is required. For example, at the height of the last property recession, I know of one architect who had real problems with payments from his clients and on one occasion he literally stood over one of them while they wrote him a cheque. Without this, he wouldn't have been able to pay his staff; drastic action, but absolutely necessary.

So when it comes to getting paid and on time, remember to:

- do everything you can to ensure you get paid on time;
- establish firm rules for credit control for when you don't get paid on time;
- where necessary, take legal action to recover your debts.

Do everything you can to ensure you get paid on time

In every business and especially small and medium-sized enterprises, cash is king. Keeping the cash flowing into your business is essential, so make sure you make it easy for customers to pay you. Here are some basic ground rules to bear in mind (you may need to vary them according to who you are working with, as some may be more applicable than others).

- Set out your standard terms and conditions of sale up front. These should include payment terms and any penalties for late payment, such as the imposition of interest. When you agree to work for a client, ask them to sign an assignment letter (or similar) which demonstrates they've received and accepted your terms and conditions. Then if there's any dispute you can refer back to the terms and conditions they agreed to. Without these, you have very little basis for negotiation. With respect to payment terms, these are typically set at 30 days, which shows just how bad late paying has become in the UK. However, there' no need to stick to this if you don't want to – some freelancers request payment within 14 days. If you need some help setting up your terms and conditions, a solicitor is a good place to start and there are quite a few websites where you can download pre-defined terms and conditions to suit your business for a small fee (see Useful Links at the back of the book).
- Keep your invoices simple so that they're easily understood and, of course, accurate (as mentioned above). This will reduce the likelihood of a query which only delays payment.
- Undertake credit checks. Although this might seem extreme, it can save you a lot of problems down the line. A credit check will reveal how good a payer your client is and if they're known to be poor, it may be worth you not working with them unless they provide you with some cast-iron guarantees that they'll pay. You could also ask for some payment upfront to reduce your risk. In general, it's a good idea to perform credit checks on all new clients, but do use your judgement: if you start working for a large blue-chip company, for example, it'll

probably be unnecessary. In these instances, you should apply good credit controls (see next section). Credit checks are relatively inexpensive (and certainly worth the money to avoid you getting a nasty surprise when you're expecting a large cheque), but the costs can mount up, so it may be worth setting some limits on the size of sale so that you don't end up eating into your profits.

- Set credit limits. If you're going to be working with one client for some time, you could establish a credit limit which they must not exceed. This allows you to manage the risk of working for long periods of time without getting paid. To be effective, you need to discuss the limit at the time of the sale or contract negotiation and also decide on what action you might take if it's exceeded. Clearly the option to withdraw your services if you're not getting paid is one worth considering, but you should exercise this with caution as you may run the risk of not being paid at all.

- Offer discounts for early payment. This approach should be used sparingly, so that clients don't start to expect a discount from you every time. A lot depends on how quickly you want to be paid and the size of the assignment. For example, if you want payment within seven days, you could offer a 10 per cent discount.

- Seek references where appropriate. In some instances, you might want to ask your client for a small number of supplier references whom you can contact so that you can satisfy yourself that they are good payers. Naturally, if these are provided by the client themselves they'll only be positive, so should be treated as the 'best case' scenario.

■ Request direct payment into your bank account. This is a great way to avoid any problems associated with that old chestnut 'the cheque's in the post', and will also be quick for your client to process, which is always a good idea. The other benefit is that wired funds are automatically cleared, so you can access your money immediately.

Establish firm rules for credit control for when you don't get paid on time

Even though you may make it easy for your clients to pay you, most people have a relatively poor track record for paying on time, so you'll need to have a solid credit-control process in place to sort things out. As a general rule, the longer you leave an outstanding debt, the harder it is to resolve. Organisations rarely pay an overdue debt without reminders, so it's in your best interests to chase any outstanding invoices. Here are a few things you should consider when dealing with your creditors. As you'll see, there's a built-in escalation route.

■ Whenever an invoice becomes overdue, make sure you follow it up within a day or two and don't be tempted to leave it. Whatever you do, don't feel guilty about making a fuss: after all, it's money owed to you. Problems can often be resolved very quickly by a polite e-mail, phone call or both.

■ Make sure you establish a single point of contact within your client's accounts department with whom you can discuss invoicing issues. This is good practice whether you have to deal with late payments or not: it's always useful to develop a good relationship with someone rather than have to deal with a 'faceless' e-mail address.

- Ask the person who commissioned you to speak to accounts on your behalf. I use this approach quite a lot because it provides some internal pressure on the problem, and if the client likes you, they'll want to keep you as happy as you keep them.

- Unless you're operating as a sole trader, ask someone else in your company to chase your debts. This will help you maintain a good relationship with your main client contact.

- Try to get to the bottom of why the invoice has not been paid. Have they lost it, for example? Was it incorrect, or is there an issue with the services you've provided? Or has the client run into difficulties? It's always a good idea to find out why before you take any further action: there may be a simple explanation for the late payment.

- If you're getting nowhere, it's best to follow up with a formal letter. Remind your client of the issue and be prepared to quote your terms and conditions and, if necessary, demand that interest is paid on the outstanding invoice. The Late Payment of Commercial Debts (Interest) Act 1998 allows small businesses to claim interest on overdue payments from other companies and small businesses. The Act assumes that a payment is late after 30 days and permits you to charge 8 per cent above the prevailing Bank of England base rate. And to avoid any doubt, it's well worth quoting the Act in any correspondence. It may get a little messy, but if you have to use the weight of the legal system to get paid then so be it. And if a client is that bad at paying, you'll probably never want to work with them again anyway, so you have nothing to lose.

■ Some organisations name and shame those companies that are poor payers by pointing them out on their website. Extreme perhaps, but it sends out a message, and in an age where reputation matters, this can be an effective approach to adopt.

Taking legal action to recover your debts

It is a sad fact that in some cases, it'll be necessary to take legal action to recover your debts. This is never easy and it can be expensive, so do think about the costs associated with this route before you embark on it. If the outstanding debt is low, you may consider writing it off, although I would only do this if all other routes have either been exhausted or are not worth pursuing. If you need to follow a legal route, the typical steps are:

■ issue a 'Letter Before Action' which informs your client of what you want and why. The letter will need to include details of the invoices which have yet to be paid and a warning that if the money isn't paid within seven days, court proceedings may start. This may be all that's needed, as it demonstrates to your client that you're serious about what's owed to you and that you're willing to follow through with legal action, if needed, to secure payment.

- if the client still doesn't pay, seek a legal solution through the courts. If the amount is small (typically £5,000 or less), you can use the Small Claims Court to settle the issue. If it's more, it's worth employing a solicitor who'll help you pursue your claim. In both cases, extra costs will be incurred, but if you win your claim, your costs will be paid by the defendant.
- The debtor will have 28 days to pay the judgement debt (issued by the court) and if they fail to pay, a County Court Judgement (CCJ) will be served against them and entered on to the County Court Judgement Register. This will remain with the debtor for six years and will have a significant impact on their ability to raise credit. It will also, of course, feature on any future credit checks which may be made by other suppliers.
- The last resort involves the use of bailiffs and High Court enforcement officers to recover the debt. Thankfully this is quite rare and if it should happen, it will be managed by the court.

Finally, it's often worth considering using a specialist debt collection agency that specialises in credit management and debt collection. If you decide to use an agency, make sure you do your homework and choose one that you're happy to work with and remember you'll have to pay for their services, either as a fee to cover the cost of the recovery (which can be a few hundred pounds), or as a percentage of the debt recovered.

Managing your creditors is an important part of your financial management activities and although we may not like it, we have little choice – it's part of the deal in becoming a freelance employee. However, there are plenty of things you *can* do to make it easier for your clients to pay and you should use everything at your disposal to do so. From my experience, most problems with billing can be resolved quickly and amicably, but you need to be prepared on the odd occasion to use more draconian methods to ensure you get paid. You owe it to yourself and your future business – you're not a charity! The good thing is that when a client sees that you're prepared to follow through, they usually pay up.

Of course, there are a few other issues which can have a big impact on your financial health and it is to these we can now turn.

Avoiding the cliff and other hazards

One of the things about being a freelancer is that there are many more traps and hazards to avoid than if you're a full-time employee. Some are perhaps more obvious than others and it's likely that some people fall prey to them due to lack of experience. In other cases, though, these problems crop up because of a lack of planning or a poor grasp of what a freelance career actually entails. And like most things associated with a freelance career, the pitfalls usually have some kind of financial consequence to them.

The commodity trap

In 2007 I finished writing my book *Commoditization and the Strategic Response*, in which I explored the impacts of changes in technology, knowledge, demographics and competition on the world of work and on what you and I get paid. It was clear that there's a downward trend in incomes for many of us and especially those who have what could be considered to be commodity skills. Let's look at one example.

About 10 years ago, I was a project manager in a government agency working on various IT projects for the business. Being a project manager was special; there was some kudos attached to the title, as the skills, knowledge and expertise were quite limited and restricted to relatively few specialists. Project managers could earn decent salaries and could expect to do so well into the future. But things have changed since then. Project managers, although still critical to many organisations are more common, cost less, and the kudos attached to the title has diminished considerably. In fact most project managers prefer to be called programme managers these days because of the status that programme managers have over project managers. Why has this happened? There are a few reasons.

First, the number of qualified project managers has increased significantly – no wonder when the demand for their skills has grown as organisational complexity and the need for effective change has increased. The basics of supply and demand have meant that project managers can now be hired more cheaply than in the past. Second, professional bodies, academics and practitioners alike have strived to improve the quality and repeatability of the underlying processes of project management, thereby opening them up to the forces of commoditisation. The introduction of detailed standards, processes and a proliferation of courses which train people to the same level all help to demystify the art of project management and lower the bar to entry. In essence it has allowed much of the tacit knowledge of experienced project managers to be distilled and codified so that it can become explicit and reusable. Finally, the increasing use of technology, aided and abetted by this codification, has reduced some of the toil and intellectual horsepower required to execute the project-management processes. Some argue that it releases the project manager to do more value-added work and concentrate on leadership and direction. Others believe that it's dumbed down the role of project manager, or has at least allowed the process of project management to be undertaken by someone who's lesser qualified, more junior and ultimately cheaper to employ.

There are many other examples besides the one above, and it's important to consider whether or not the skills and competencies you bring to your clients are easily replicated and hence only capable of commanding a lower daily rate. Commoditisation is a very real threat to every freelancer and it's comparatively straightforward to identify the early warning signs, which include among others:

- a belief that all suppliers are fundamentally the same;
- an increasing preference for customers to select on the basis of price and little else;

■ a reluctance for customers to pay for anything they consider unnecessary;

■ increasing pressures on margins (in other words your income).

Key to avoiding the trap of commoditisation is to make sure the skills and capabilities you have are not only current and in demand, but ideally difficult to replicate. In the past, this was a lot simpler for two reasons. First, the number of people who may have had similar skills and capabilities as you was probably a lot lower than it is today. Second, many of the skills and capabilities which are now considered commoditisable were unlikely to have been so in the past. The ability to codify work is now a lot simpler and there's nothing to suggest that this process of codification will slow in the foreseeable future. To succeed as a freelancer, where many of the skills and capabilities which we use now will have become commoditisable activities in the future, you'll need to ensure you maintain a weather eye on the broader market in which you sell your services. To that end, it's a good idea to make a simple assessment of your skills, as this will help you determine where your value comes from – essential if you're going to maximise your income[1]. Consider the following three groups of skills:

[1] Stewart, T. (1997), *Intellectual Capital: The New Wealth of Nations*, New York: Currency-Doubleday, p. 89

1 **COMMODITY SKILLS.** These are skills that are general to any role or business. They can be picked up quickly by most people and are increasingly easy to codify. They include following processes, as well as other types of skill, such as technical maintenance and machine minding (as in a factory), call-centre work, reviewing X-rays, and most forms of transaction processing such as accounts payable or auditing. We all need commodity skills, as do organisations, but to maximise your earnings and gain the most satisfaction in your work you need to move beyond these

2 **LEVERAGED SKILLS.** These are skills that are non-company specific, more complex and typically have a higher value attached to them and may be considered more valuable to some clients than others. The ability to synthesise would fall into this category, for example. Although many organisations may have similar skills internally, they're often unable to make use of them when required, plus they're not always able to break through the barriers to change, such as politics and resistance. This is why clients are willing to pay good rates to freelancers

3 **PROPRIETARY SKILLS.** These are the skills and knowledge that are company specific and which a company will pay a premium for because they translate into the wider company brand. Think of Coca Cola, Disney, Mercedes Benz and similar companies. Each develops and utilises their unique blend of skills to create products and services that command respect and loyalty among their customers. In a similar vein, there are skills and knowledge which are valued in the workplace which you may

possess and for which you can command a premium. It's important, however, to recognise that such skills are company specific, and although this doesn't mean they're not portable, they do have to be repackaged to suit a new client. This is principally because each organisation has its own way of doing things defined by its culture, and in order to fit in you'll need to make the effort to adapt to the new environment.

Taking on unnecessary costs

When you move into freelance work, there is an overriding temptation to set yourself up so that everything is ready on day one and everyone can see that you're established. Taking on new office space is probably the number one expenditure which a large number of freelancers think about, and especially those who move into any form of professional services, such as law, accountancy and consultancy. But without a solid revenue stream, such things can be a significant drain on your income and may result in you struggling to get by at best, or giving up and moving back into the mainstream workforce at worst. Therefore, it's a good idea to avoid as many of the fixed costs as possible, be that a new or leased car or office space. Particularly in the early days, I consider commercial office space a luxury unless it's absolutely necessary. Use hotel reception/meeting areas for business meetings or your client's offices. Or, if you need space for a workshop, use a hotel meeting room, or facilities from companies like Regus that will hire out high-quality rooms and office on very short lets. Naturally, as your business develops and you become more confident about the predictability of the revenue streams, securing premises and getting a new car are things which you can do without spoiling your long-term future. With respect to premises, the good thing is that many people today work from home or out of short-term let managed offices which are by far and away the cheaper option. And remember you're not judged on your car or office in most cases, it's the value you add to your customers that matters.

Never taking a holiday

This seems to be one of the biggest issues for the freelance worker. Although many people move into freelance work to get a much better work–life balance or to work around family commitments, quite a number seem to slip into some bad habits, one of which is never to take a holiday. A few years ago I was working with a freelance project manager. He was a nice guy, competent and was earning a handsome rate for that time – something like £800 per day. We were working on a major change programme and like many large initiatives, the hours were long. When it came to taking a holiday, he did nothing but complain about the financial implications of taking a few days off. His main concern was his loss of earnings. He would moan about how each day would cost him £800 and on top of that he had to pay for the holiday as well. It was almost that he begrudged taking any time off. I couldn't understand him then and I still can't now. As someone who was earning significantly more than the average employee, he was more than able to suffer the nominal loss of earnings and yet he was so obsessed about the opportunity costs that he just continued to work.

Avoiding this common pitfall is quite simple and requires you to develop a different attitude to taking a holiday than the one our project manager had. First, you need to be aware of the psychological and physical benefits of having a break. Not having any time off – and by 'time off' I mean more than just the occasional day here and there – can have financial implications down the line. If you are tired, burnt out and generally fatigued, you won't be performing at your best and your reputation might suffer. Not only that, but you're more likely to make mistakes and become ill, which could have a major impact on your earning ability. Taking time off is very important and makes economic sense. Second, and in order to make it easy for you to take a holiday, you need to set your target income for the year (as mentioned in Chapter 1). This should cover your living costs and expenses for the year and should also cover holidays and possibly the chance that you may have to take some time off because you're unwell. As long as your earnings are on track, there's no excuse for not taking a holiday. Next, take the same view of holidays as you probably did when you were a full-time employee, and assume they're simply part and parcel of your working year. And finally, don't think about your holidays as a loss of income because that will spoil your break. It's far better to think of a holiday as a well-deserved rest which has nothing to do with earning a living. So cut yourself some slack and take that holiday – you'll benefit from it in the long term.

Falling off 'the cliff'

Another major hazard for the freelancer is what is euphemistically called 'the cliff', and this one can have significant financial implications. Many freelancers, and especially those who are new to the freelance world, tend to focus exclusively on their current work contract, as you'd expect them to. However, focusing on your current assignment without keeping an eye on the future can lead to problems when the contract has ended; you may find yourself without any work and insufficient funds to tide you over until the next assignment comes along (there's more on this in Chapter 9). A former colleague at PricewaterhouseCoopers fell into this trap. He left his employer a couple of years ago for a freelance career, only to find himself without any work once his assignment had finished. As he told me, he spent all his time working on his initial contract and had failed to carve out any time to generate his next assignment. Having finished the first assignment, he struggled to find a new contract and as the money began to dry up, decided to return to mainstream employment.

This is a common problem and many freelancers' dreams of never having to work for someone else again are shattered as a result. Avoiding it requires a lot of focus and effort and necessitates building up your network, generating sales and seeking opportunities to promote what you do (something we touched on in Chapters 4 and 5). Clearly the cliff is a common hazard which freelancers have to face and most of us have to deal with the occasional cliff, even if it's quite small. The cliff tends to be less of a problem for those freelancers that source their work from agencies because the agency should be looking for new work on your behalf all the time (after all, that's how they get paid).

Becoming too isolated

Working on a freelance basis often means that you'll be spending a lot of time on your own and very often at home. This can be quite hard to deal with, especially if you've come from employment where you spent all day with lots of other people and as a result have been used to having company. Although it can be quite novel to begin with, many freelancers struggle with the feelings of isolation at least some of the time. In extreme cases, some even give up freelancing because they find they miss other people too much. Dealing with the isolation can be relatively straightforward, if you choose to plan your working days appropriately. And remember, one of the benefits of freelance work is that it places you in control, which means you're able to structure your day in a way that best suits you. I know plenty of freelancers who'll build in opportunities to meet people and socialise in order to combat the feelings of loneliness.

Typical ways to eliminate the isolation include arranging to meet friends during the working week; attending lectures and other similar events where you can meet other people, and going to the gym during the day. I usually play badminton on a Friday morning for a couple of hours and I even know of one freelancer who goes to the pub or a cafe once or twice a week just to be near people. The key to combating isolation is to be creative and to remember that you don't have to be chained to your desk all day long. Remember, you are in control and once you get used to spending more time on your own, it will become easier to cope with.

Failing to network

I explained the importance and some of the dos and don'ts of networking in Chapter 5, so there's no need for huge amounts of detail here. However, as a pitfall, failing to network can be significant and can be one of the causes of the hazard of the cliff mentioned above. To be a successful freelancer requires that you maintain a network of business contacts, one of your main sources of future work, in fact, but keeping in regular contact with potential clients needn't be arduous. You'll need to ensure you don't pester your contacts – depending on how many contacts you choose to maintain, networking should be part of your daily or weekly routine.

Taking on too much and working non-stop

Overloading yourself with work and developing workaholic tendencies is an all-too-common occurrence for freelancers. It can, of course, equally apply to full-time employees, but one of the reasons it tends to be particularly prevalent among freelancers is that they're acutely aware that they've no safety blankets and understand that if they're not working, they're not earning. It is easy, therefore, to say 'yes' to every opportunity and find yourself over-committing to your clients. Over time, this can lead to burn-out and may even lead you to seek mainstream employment where the pressures may be less severe. Key to steering clear of this pitfall involves saying 'no' when it's necessary. Rather than take on work you may not enjoy or just won't make any money from, at times, you'll have to be quite hard-nosed about things and not worry about possibly offending someone. If you're offered a job, always look at the financial margin you're likely to generate after taking out all of your costs. Once you've done this, you can assess the value of the opportunity before saying 'yes'. This will allow you to make best use of your time and spend it on more productive activities. Another technique which will help you to avoid the tendency of overworking is to establish a set number of hours you'll work every week. Although this will vary according to the deadlines you face, it does allow you to keep your working hours to an acceptable level. It can sometimes even help enhance your reputation to say 'no' to work as clients then perceive you to be in demand.

Failing to seek help when you need it

Always be prepared to pay for advice. As a freelancer, it often feels as though you have to do everything yourself, and it can be difficult to ask for advice when you want to be self-sufficient. However, it's always a good idea to seek out advice in those areas where you're less confident or which fall outside of your area of expertise. For example, as frequently stressed elsewhere, it's a good idea to consider using an accountant to run your basic monthly business accounts as well as your annual accounts, payroll and tax advice. They can do the job more quickly and accurately than you and, more importantly, using an accountant will free up your time so you can spend it on doing what you are good at and developing your business.

An accountant will also help keep you on top of that all-important aspect of business control, cash management. Apart from using the expertise of an accountant, there may be the occasional need to seek the input of other professionals, such as marketers, sales experts and solicitors. All can bring additional value as you build your business and should be considered important supports to your freelance career. Finally, don't forget other sources of input and advice, such as local chambers of commerce, the Institute of Directors and other professional and trade bodies that will keep you informed and in touch with others who are in similar positions to yourself. The most important thing is to remember that you're not alone and there are plenty of sources of input and advice available to you.

Assuming it's all going to be rosy

When you're in full-time employment, you'll have good days and bad days. When you work for yourself, in your own business, you'll extend the boundaries of both experiences. You'll feel elation when you win new business, especially in the early days. In fact, it'll be more exciting than anything you'll have experienced with your employer, especially as you know it's completely down to you and no one else can take the credit. Out will come the champagne! The other side of this is the disappointment you'll feel when business is lost. You may have worked long and hard and done everything you could to win the work but on some occasions – and for a variety of good reasons – you just won't be able to close the deal. Whatever, try not to panic or be overwhelmed by bad news. It'll only sap your energy and, if you're not careful, lead you into a negative spiral. All you can do is pick yourself up, reflect on the experience and get on with creating the next opportunity. While it's easy to rely on just one client, it's not sensible and you'll be vulnerable when they no longer require your services. Setbacks are part of the freelance life and being able to get over them is a skill you have to develop.

Navigating your way through a freelance career can be both fun and scary, especially in the early days. Avoiding as many of the pitfalls as possible during the first couple of years is important, and once you've successfully negotiated these, you'll be well and truly on the way to a successful freelance career.

The joy of tax

Tax is perhaps one of the most contentious issues for the freelancer. It's often fraught with difficulties, but especially for those new to self-employment. And let's face it, none of us likes to pay tax, although it's unavoidable.

This chapter covers as many of the tax issues facing the freelancer as possible, but it's essential that you also seek professional advice tailored to your circumstances from an accountant or business adviser, such as Business Link. There are a few simple reasons for this. First, falling foul of Her Majesty's Revenue & Customs (HMRC) can be both time-consuming and expensive (see later in this chapter for just what it entails), so you'd better make sure that you pay what's due and on time. Second, tax law changes so often that it's better to pay for the services of someone who's an expert in the field than to try to keep abreast of the changes yourself; your time will be better spent on generating new business and adding value to your clients. And finally, there are plenty of legitimate ways of reducing your tax liability on which only an expert will be best placed to advise you. Key to dealing with tax, like so many things in a freelance career, requires a combination of discipline, accurate record-keeping and being on top of deadlines. And, once you get used to it, you'll find that tax isn't as bad as you may have thought.

Tax for the freelancer can be broken down into that which is associated with the company and that which relates to personal income. Of course, for many these are one and the same, but how and when tax is paid will vary and your company structure will have an impact on it (see Chapter 2 to remind yourself about how tax is treated). And you do have to be careful because HMRC is acutely aware of the approaches used by freelancers to reduce tax; in many cases, they've now eliminated those that they considered to be unjust, for example paying yourself a very low salary and then taking multiples of your salary in dividends to avoid paying tax. HMRC now expects your dividends to be commensurable with your salary otherwise they see this as tax avoidance. So, in addition to dealing with company and personal tax, this chapter covers some of the major areas of tax legislation that the freelancer has to contend with, such as IR35, as well as explaining what to expect if you're investigated by HMRC.

Company taxation

There are three kinds of tax that your company will be subject to:

1   **CORPORATION TAX (CT).** As mentioned in Chapter 2, all
    limited companies are subject to corporation tax which is charged at
    21 per cent for small businesses (up to profits of £300,000) and
    28 per cent for larger businesses with profits in excess of £1,500,000.
    Some tax relief is available to growing businesses as they move from the
    small companies' rate to the main rate. Unless you happen to be
    exceptionally well paid, then most freelancers will be subject to the small
    companies' rate.

2   **NATIONAL INSURANCE (NI).** If you're running your business as a
    limited company, you'll be required to pay employers' National Insurance
    which is payable on your gross income at a rate of 12.8 per cent.
    Employers' National Insurance is paid monthly and forms part of the
    deductions that you see on your payslip, and is probably something you
    never paid any attention to when you were a full-time employee. You'll also
    be paying employees' National Insurance too, but the amount you actually
    end up paying will depend on how much you choose to pay yourself in
    salary and how much in dividends (see later).

3   **VALUE ADDED TAX (VAT).** This tax is charged on most business
    transactions made in the UK. It's also charged on goods and some
    services imported from places outside the European Union and on goods
    and some services coming into the UK from the other EU countries. All
    goods and services that are VAT rated are called 'taxable supplies' and
    you must charge VAT on your taxable supplies from the date you first

need to be registered. The value of these supplies is called your 'taxable turnover'. Although you don't have to be VAT registered if the turnover of your business is below £67,000 (2008–2009 figure), there are some advantages of doing so. Registering for VAT allows you to claim back 17.5 per cent of the goods and services you purchase as part of running your business, so it makes sense for most freelancers to register. Naturally, should the turnover of your business increase to the point where it reaches or exceeds the threshold, you'll be required to register anyway. In essence, you're collecting tax on behalf of HMRC and as such you'll have to provide a VAT return to them each quarter. It's possible to make the VAT process a little simpler by opting for the flat-rate scheme. With this, you make monthly or quarterly instalments towards your annual VAT bill (based upon your predicted turnover) and then submit a single return at the end of the year, with any outstanding balance that may be due.

The amount of tax you pay can be reduced by offsetting your allowable expenses. Your accountant or HMRC will be able to provide you with the rules associated with expenses, but these typically include rent and overheads for the premises (which includes your home office) that you use for running your company, equipment such as machinery and computers, stationery, and any vehicles you may use for the business (not for your personal use, however).

Dividends

A good number of freelancers tend to operate under the umbrella of a limited company because it offers some major tax advantages over the sole-trader or partnership models. The principal advantage lies in paying yourself a low salary (near your annual tax-free allowance, which for 2008–2009 is £6,035) and augmenting your income with company dividends that are subject to lower tax (10 per cent if you're a basic-rate taxpayer and 32.5 per cent if you're a higher-rate taxpayer) and there's no NI to pay. This is possible because the company is a separate legal entity and is recognised under the law as being separate from the shareholders who own it. Assuming that your contract doesn't fall under the IR35 tax legislation (see below), you're able to distribute the after-tax profits from your business as dividends. Dividends can be taken at any time and as often as you like *as long as* they're paid from company profits after corporation tax (currently 19 per cent) has been set aside or paid. It's important to remember that dividends can't be greater than the company's profits and their distribution must follow a set protocol and be appropriately documented. You accountant can help you with this. If you run your business with your spouse or civil partner, you'll also need to consider the implications of the changes associated with the S660 legislation (see below).

Personal tax

If you're new to freelancing and have come from an organisation which has paid you direct, it's probably unlikely that you'll have worried that much about your tax position, apart from seeing tax automatically disappearing from your payslip each month. For most people, this changes when they become a freelance employee. When you become self-employed, you'll typically have to complete an annual self-assessment tax return. This is something that anyone who's considered to have complex tax affairs or is a higher-rate taxpayer has to complete each year. Naturally, if your limited company is very small and has a low turnover, you'll still pay yourself using the Pay As You Earn (PAYE) system, so much of the tax administration resides at the company level (which you or your accountant will still have to comply with).

If, like many freelancers, you need to complete an annual self-assessment return to HMRC, it isn't as daunting as it might first seem. The self-assessment mechanism has been around for a long time now, but if you find it too much, you can always have your accountant complete it on your behalf which will cost a few hundred pounds.

You'll need to complete an annual return for each tax year (this runs from 6 April one year to 5 April the following year). The return, along with any tax due, must be with HMRC by 31 January the year *after* the end of the tax year. So for example, the 2009/10 tax year starts on 6 April 2009 and ends on 5 April 2010. Any tax due will need to be paid by 31 January 2011. Stick to the deadlines as far as possible, as there are penalties for late payments which can also include interest on any outstanding tax due if the delay is significant. HMRC is increasingly coming down much harder on later payers, so pay on time.

If you prefer, you can have HMRC calculate the tax due for you. If you go for this option, you'll need to have your return completed by 30 September after the end of the tax year. Submitting your tax return online can make savings and help with calculations, if you decide to do it yourself.

In addition to paying the tax due, you'll also need to make payments on account every six months. The idea behind this is that you can keep on top of your taxes throughout the year and when you submit your assessment the following year there should be no tax to pay. It also assumes that your income will be the same for the following tax year. Should your income change over the course of the year, you may end up paying some additional tax or be due a refund. The instalments for each tax year are due on 31 January (when you pay the tax you owe for the previous tax year) and 31 July. For example, if you had to pay £14,000 in tax in the 2008/09 tax year, you'd need to pay £7,000 as the first instalment for the 2009/10 tax year on 31 January and then another £7,000 on 31 July. Naturally, the actual amount will depend on your income, but the key thing is to remember that if you're self-employed (as a partner or sole trader), and hence not PAYE, you'll need to pay some tax up front; it's just a way for HMRC to smooth out your payments and to ensure they collect tax from you more than once per year. Assuming you set your tax aside, this should present no problems. It's possible to apply to reduce the instalments on account if you expect your income will be lower the following year, but if it isn't you'll be charged interest by HMRC.

If you've been used to having all things tax-related taken care of by your previous employer, taking control of it all can be a shock. Freelancers are often caught on the hop when they forget to set aside money to pay for next year's tax bill. And depending on when you start your life as a freelance employee, it might be some time before you actually do pay any tax. For example, if you started out on 1 May 2007, you may not have to pay any tax until 31 January 2009. At this point, tax on *17 months' income* will be due. There are also a couple of other issues to think about, if you become a partner. The first has to do with National Insurance contributions (NICs) which are Class 2 for the self-employed and require weekly payments of £2.30. This is usually collected quarterly. If you're a sole trader or a partner, you'll also be liable for Class 4 NI payments on any profits taken out of the business. These payments are made on profits between the lower and upper profits limit as set by HMRC and updated each tax year (currently these are £5,435 and £40,040 respectively). The rate at which Class 4 NI is paid is currently 8 per cent and there's an additional 1 per cent charge on all profits above the upper profits limit.

Keeping on top of tax legislation and investigations

Sometimes it feels as though we do nothing but pay more and more tax. And whether tax is collected directly or indirectly, it's been a while since tax rates have genuinely come down. Chancellors may grab the headlines by announcing to the general public that the headline rate of tax has been reduced, but it's only once the detailed legislation has been analysed that the full impacts and increases are truly known. No surprise, then, that accountants and tax experts aim to find effective and legitimate ways to reduce the tax liabilities of their clients. And it should equally come as no surprise that HMRC does its best to close any loopholes the accountants and tax experts find. Two examples are especially pertinent to the self employed – IR35 and Section 660.

IR35

Although IR35 has now been around for some time, it still courts plenty of controversy within the contracting and freelance communities. The legislation, which was introduced in 1999 and took effect in April 2000, allows to tax some contractors as though they were employees of their clients. This addresses one of their biggest concerns about contractors who work for the same company year after year and who are, to all intents and purposes, employees. As mentioned earlier, I used to know freelancers who would outlast permanent staff and earn significantly more than their full-time colleagues.

HMRC believed that many freelancers were, in fact, avoiding paying tax and NI through the use of intermediaries such as personal services companies. Such firms were used to obtain work with their clients directly or indirectly through agencies, even though the contractor was the only employee. HMRC argued that if the company were removed, the contractor could be deemed to be an employee of the agency or client and as such, be liable for the same levels of tax and NI as a full-time employee. Before the legislation was introduced, a freelancer could avoid being taxed as an employee on payments for services by providing his or her services through the service company. The freelancer then could take the money out of the service company in the form of dividends instead of a salary. As dividends aren't liable for NI payments, the freelancer paid less NI than either an employee or a self-employed person and on top of that PAYE tax is not applicable to dividends. As you'd expect, the impact on freelancers' incomes was sufficiently large to cause an outcry; in some cases it meant a 25 per cent reduction.

All freelancers need to be aware of the implications of IR35 and to understand whether or not they fall within its definition. Because it's not clear-cut, it's important to check the terms of the contract under which you work and also your working arrangements and conditions. As a rule of thumb, you're likely to fall under IR35 if:

- you work set hours, or a given number of hours a week or a month in the same way that an employee would;
- you have to do the work yourself rather than hire someone else to do the work for you;
- your client is able to tell you what to do, when to work and how to execute the assignment – that is, they're in control in the same way a line manager would be;

- you're paid by the hour, week or month;
- you're entitled to paid over-time;
- you have to work at the client's premises or at a place or places determined by them;
- you work for one client at a time, rather than having a number of contracts with different clients.

If you're able to answer 'yes' to most of the questions above, you're more like an employee than a freelancer. On the other hand, you're *less* likely to be impacted by IR35 if:

- you have the final say in how you do the work for the client;
- you could potentially make a loss on the contract;
- you provide the main items of equipment you need to do the job for the client;
- you are free to hire other people on your own terms to support you in the execution of the contract – in other words, paying them yourself;
- you're responsible for the quality of the outputs and for any rework;
- you have multiple clients.

In the end, there are a number of factors you'll need to bear in mind when drawing up your contract. As always, it's extremely important that you seek professional advice if you're unclear about whether or not you fall within the boundaries of IR35.

THE JOY OF TAX

Section 660 (S660)

Although the tax rules associated with settlement legislation 660 (also known as S660) are certainly not new, having been around since the 1930s, their application to small businesses is. The original legislation was designed to prevent the passing of income or assets to other family members in order to reduce the overall tax bill (or 'settling', as it's known). Today, the tax law is being refocused on husband and wife and civil partnership-run businesses and is aimed at preventing income sharing or shifting. In such companies, a husband and wife may each own an equal number of shares, even though the work undertaken by each is uneven. For example, one of them would be the main fee earner and the other would either bring in a very small proportion of the overall fees or would undertake work for a small amount of income.

The problem HMRC has with this is not so much what people do, but how the company dividends are shared out. When the profits are paid out by way of dividend, income earned by the primary fee earner can be partly received by the other, who is also taxed on it, resulting in an overall saving on tax since both the husband and wife can make the most of their personal allowance and basic-rate tax bands. This approach to income sharing is believed to be used by up to 300,000 husband-and-wife businesses and, up until fairly recently, this was considered to be an acceptable approach to tax planning.

The issue has been bubbling away for a few years as a result of HMRC's pursuit of a particular husband and wife business (Arctic Systems). Their argument was that the wife's dividends didn't reflect her contribution to the business, as the husband brought in most of its income. As a result, the business would fall under the rules of S660. The husband and wife were taken to court and although they lost both the initial case and the High Court appeal, they took their case to the House of Lords who found in their favour. As a result of the defeat, and despite the support for husband and wife-run businesses across the political and corporate spectrum, HMRC rewrote the tax law associated with income-splitting arrangements and is expected to introduce these new measures in April 2009. Under the new legislation, taxpayers will have to detail how much income they've foregone by making a comparison with how the business would have operated, had all their work been done independently on a fully commercial basis. As with IR35, it's essential to understand how S660 could impact your business, especially if you work with your spouse or civil partner.

Tax investigations

As the ability to increase the overall tax take gets harder, HMRC is becoming increasingly focused on reducing the currently high levels of tax avoidance. When you consider that between 2000 and 2005 some £41 billion of direct taxes has been lost through avoidance, you can see why it's putting its energies into recovering as much of it as possible. As a result of the 2008 Finance Bill, HMRC is seeking to increase its powers so that it's able to make unannounced inspections of a business's and individual's tax records. If it's approved, it's highly likely that the number of investigations will increase. Even if you're abiding by all the tax rules applicable to you and your business, investigations still occur and remain a worrying, time-consuming and often expensive process. There are in essence two types of review:

1 **BUSINESS REVIEWS.** HMRC uses sophisticated modelling techniques to identify businesses which might be avoiding tax (taxi drivers and fast-food joints are particular favourites because much of their business is cash based and therefore easier to hide). You might find your company being investigated if HMRC is finding issues with similar businesses; if there are errors on tax returns; if they've been tipped off by a competitor; after a review of the business's tax file, or, of course, because your company has been selected completely randomly.

2 **SELF-ASSESSMENT REVIEWS.** From a freelancer's perspective, these might arise from a suspicion that you fall under IR35 but aren't declaring it (for example, you're receiving round sums of income from the same client which may indicate that you're receiving the same income each month); a business review has identified payments to a contractor who's not registered as such on HMRC databases; or if your income and expenses vary from other freelancers in your field.

If you ever find yourself the subject of an investigation, there are a few cardinal rules. First and foremost, co-operate and help the inspectors complete their investigation as smoothly and quickly as possible. This is likely to involve providing copies of business documents such as invoices, and depending on what the investigation reveals, an interview which can last for a few hours. Second, seek out professional support and advice from your accountant who'll be better placed to handle the inspection than you. Despite the additional cost, it's generally worth it as they're used to HMRC investigations. And finally, make sure you keep your records up to date, always pay your taxes when they're due and comply with the latest tax legislation. On average, businesses should expect to be investigated every five to six years, so it's well worth planning ahead. With respect to self-assessment investigations, these can occur at any time although they're comparatively rare.

And, finally, don't forget to save for your taxes

My cousin is a freelance project manager in Canada and he's usually gainfully employed. However, the one thing that he mentioned to me the last time he was between contracts was that he had to pay a large tax bill using his credit card. So he was paying interest on a debt that wouldn't have been necessary, had he put aside cash to cover the tax he was anticipating on paying. Of course, I thought this was an isolated example of poor planning, but it seems that this isn't the case. According to one study at least, the vast majority of small businesses, and I include freelancers in this, struggle to meet their tax liabilities at the end of the year. Despite all the advice, the majority of small businesses fail to set aside sufficient funds to pay their tax and around a fifth save nothing at all. This is a huge mistake which should be avoided because you'll end up paying interest and late payments unnecessarily. If you're one of the sensible freelancers who's diligent in setting aside the money due for tax, you can make it work for you by putting it into a high-interest account or any other form of risk-free investment which can be accessed when you need it. At least that way you'll be able to make some additional cash while you're waiting to pay your tax bill.

Having read this chapter you can see that there are plenty of tax-related issues you need to be on top of, which is why it's a good idea to employ an accountant. They can take away much of the perceived and real burdens associated with tax and for many freelancers it's money well spent. The other advantage is that they'll be able to advise you on how best to minimise your tax bill and ensure you comply with all the latest rules and regulations.

Assuming that you're making a good living from being a freelancer and you've covered all your taxes due, then it's worth considering some other financial matters, such as those associated with saving for your pension. This is the focus of the next chapter.

The rainy day and other personal finance issues

There's no doubt, well at least from my experience, that freelancers have a heightened sense of the importance of earning a living. Those of us who've worked or currently work within an organisation can become quite complacent about our jobs and incomes – and I count myself in this – as the money appears like clockwork every month. The only time this tends to change is when there's the threat of redundancy, but by then of course it can be too late. Now that I'm freelancing, I don't have the safety provided by my former employer which included all those things I listed in Chapter 1 and, as such, I'm even more aware that every day I'm not actively engaged with a client I'm not earning money. It certainly motivates you, and that's why being on top of invoicing and chasing late payers (see Chapter 6) is so important.

The interesting thing is that although freelancers are very concerned with the finances of their business, they often forget to worry about those which are more personal, and this has the potential to create problems in the future.

Personal finance is no different for freelancers than it is for anyone else, and let's face it there are many people in the working population who fail to take their personal finances seriously enough: negative savings rates, failure to plan for retirement, house repossessions, high levels of indebtedness and increased levels of bankruptcy suggest that personal finance is near the bottom of the list for a significant number of people. It may seem boring to worry about personal finance, but when you're sitting on a beach sipping pina colada at the end of your career, not having to worry about where your next pound is coming from, you'll value the time you spent building up your savings, no matter how dull it seemed at the time. I've also come across a large number of freelancers who tell me that they'll never retire simply because they haven't squirrelled away enough money. That's a real shame.

So, when it comes to personal finance, what should freelancers focus on? In some respects, much the same things that everyone else has to, but there are some specifics they need to worry about, mainly because there's no employer to provide all the fringe benefits mentioned in Chapter 1. In my view, there are four broad areas of personal finance on which the freelancer should focus. In order of priority, they are:

1   keeping cash for the rainy day when you may not have any work. Not only is this practical but it gives you a sense of control (and not desperation) when you're sourcing your work. It's important to be able to look for work with confidence;

2   saving for retirement, unless of course you don't want to;

3   establishing some safety nets in the form of life cover, critical illness and income replacement, as none of us is immortal and we need to think about those people we love (which includes yourself). If your partner works too, he or she will be able to get some of these benefits through their employer, so it's worth planning together to make sure that, between you, you have the kind of cover you need;

4   making sure you build up some medium-term savings and investments.

It's all too easy to procrastinate when you're faced with getting to grips with any of the above, especially those issues which seem to have no immediate benefit. But sorting yourself out now will definitely make for a more comfortable future, so let's look briefly at each of the four areas. Professional advice is essential here, as you try to work out what's best for you and your circumstances, so do take the trouble to find a good independent financial adviser. It took me a while, but it was worth the effort.

The rainy day

A few years ago, at the height of the tech bubble-induced economic slump, a good IT contractor friend of mine found himself without work. Contractors are, of course, used to periods between assignments – indeed, being able to take a break is one of the advantages that a freelance career offers – but in this case it turned out to be more than just a couple of weeks. The contract market had dried up and he found himself without work for many months. After a short while, he was soon relying on his credit cards to survive and spent a lot of time robbing Peter to pay Paul. When the market eventually started moving, he was saddled with some significant debts which took quite some time to pay off. Thankfully he managed to get back on an even keel, but he learnt a very important lesson, and that's to keep some money aside for those times when you'll be short of work and when the economic cycle changes; you might need to tide yourself over for quite some time.

So how much should you put aside for a rainy day? The general rule of thumb is to have sufficient liquid funds (i.e. cash you can lay your hands on easily) to last a minimum of six months. The actual amount of cash this represents will depend on your lifestyle, outgoings and so on. If you're more risk-averse, you might to choose to increase this to nine months or perhaps even a year. I prefer to have a little more because if things do go well, you might choose to have an extended break, which is what many freelancers do. Alternatively, if you believe that you'll rarely be short of work you could reduce the reserve to around three months, but I wouldn't go below that: three months can speed by very quickly, especially when you're looking for the next contract.

Having set your target, you then need to decide on how quickly you'll be able to reach it. Ideally you should be saving between 10 and 20 per cent of your income and placing it into a high-interest account that's separate from your day-to-day bank account. If you can reach it sooner, then even better and once it's been achieved you can focus on the other areas where you need to be targeting your personal finances. You should think carefully about where you place your cash fund, as it's well worth making it work as hard as it can for you until you need it. I tend to favour either a high-interest bank or building society account or premium bonds. The latter will tend to pay out a little less than a high-interest bank account, but there's the added excitement of potentially winning up to £1,000,000 every month. Wherever you place your rainy-day money, it should be accessible but you really must try to avoid viewing it as a pot of cash to dip into whenever you like.

Saving for retirement

The pensions industry has taken a battering over the past few years. From Equitable Life to pensions mis-selling, the papers have been full of the pitfalls and problems associated with saving for our old age. Irrespective of the problems, retirement is a major stage in everyone's lives and likely to remain so for the foreseeable future. In the UK and increasingly elsewhere, companies are cutting back on pension provision as they close down their defined benefits schemes (in which the final salary and number of years' service are used to calculate the pension that will be paid to the employee on retirement and until death) and replace these with defined contributions schemes (in which both the employer and employee contribute to a pension fund whose value at retirement depends on the level of contributions and the performance of the stock they purchase with the premiums). Such changes are driven by the aging of the population and are forcing many employees who had previously been insulated from the typical issues faced by freelancers to become more focused on their retirement and the savings needed to keep them in their dotage. This is compounded by the inability of the state to pay for our retirement; there just aren't enough young people to support an aging population. Consider the following: the number of people under 18 will fall from

7.0 to 6.6 million between now and 2011. At the same time, the proportion aged 60 and over will increase from 12.1 to 14.0 million[1]. If you're unwilling to save enough yourself, the alternatives are pretty stark; it's either a case of work until you literally drop or live off limited funds and hope they don't run out before you die. The thing about saving for retirement is that you have to start as soon as you can; there's no other choice if you want to be free to decide when you retire. Even if you fancy working for a lot longer than most other people, at least if you save enough you'll have the option to change your mind at a later date. Don't put yourself in a position where you have no choice but to work.

A few years ago, I came across a great book about retirement[2] which, although aimed at the US market, had some really helpful advice, especially the authors' 21 basic rules of retirement, some of which I've paraphrased below:

- plan far ahead and then once you have your plan, stick to it;
- invest as much as you can (see below on the current rules for retirement savings);

[1] Source: The Henley Centre

[2] Stein B. and DeMuth P. (2005), *Yes, You Can Still Retire Comfortably!*, Carlsbad, California: New Beginnings Press

- make saving for your retirement more important than looking good, driving a fast car or owning a mansion;
- don't go out and seek an amazing investment strategy that offers huge returns; instead, stick with the market and that should be sufficient;
- know that you'll be fine if you've saved too much, not too little;
- build in some flexibility should the economic conditions change and if investment approaches shift, but don't follow fads or trends.

So now that we know we've no choice but to save and have a few rules by which to abide, how much should you save and how much *can* you save? The latter is easier to answer, as this has been fixed by the government. Since the rules for pension contributions changed in 2006, a limit has been set on the total amount of pension savings (including any pension life cover) that can be used to provide benefits when you retire or die. This limit is important, because if your benefits exceed it, the excess is taxed at 55 per cent, which would come as a very nasty shock. The limit, known as the lifetime limit, was initially set at £1.5 million when the rules came into force and has been fixed up to and including the 2010/11 tax year (2007/08 – £1.6m; 2008/09 – £1.65m; 2009/10 – £1.75m; 2010/11 – £1.8m). Of course, for the majority of us, the lifetime limit is sufficiently out of reach that we probably won't have to worry. And don't forget that your pension contributions attract tax relief at source if you are a basic-rate taxpayer and through your tax code if you are a higher-rate taxpayer.

What's a little more difficult to answer is how much you need (or perhaps want) to save to allow you to retire. This isn't a simple case of coming up with a random number, as there's a range of factors to consider, such as the lifestyle you'd like to lead when you finish work, the performance of your investments, the potential impacts of inflation and so on. As a general rule, financial advisers and experts recommend that you should be aiming to replace between 60 and 80 per cent of your pre-retirement income, but the actual amount you may want will depend on such things as when you decide to retire, how long you might live for and whether you choose to phase in your retirement by continuing to work part-time, which of course after a freelance career should come naturally.

Another rule of thumb suggests that you should have saved around 12 times your annual income by the time you retire, but again the actual amount will depend on the factors previously identified. The important thing is to plan and there are plenty of pension calculators available on the Internet that can help (or worry) you. When using these calculators, don't forget that most of them assume that you're receiving pension payments from your employer, which in the case of freelancers isn't true. This means that you might need to save nearer 20 per cent of your monthly income.

Of course, it's possible to arrange for your company to pay your pension and, depending on the company structure you choose (see Chapter 2), this can be a tax-efficient way to transfer income at source into your pension. You should speak to your accountant if you have one, as they should provide you with the advice you need to determine the most tax-efficient way to save for your retirement. They and your financial adviser may even recommend having a self-invested personal pension (SIPP). A SIPP allows you to have more control over where and how your money is invested. So unlike handing your money over to an insurance company or a fund manager, you're able to take control and broaden your investment decisions, by investing in stocks and shares, unit trusts, managed funds and property. As with any decision associated with your future, you should seek advice to assess whether or not a SIPP is right for you.

Setting up some safety nets

As discussed in Chapter 1, being a freelancer means giving up some of the perks of working for an employer that offers a whole range of benefits which protect you, your income and your family. For example, suffering a major illness while employed is never a pleasant experience, especially if it's for an extended period of time or involves a stay in hospital. When this happens to a full-time employee, their employer will usually cover their income for a while, allow time off for medical appointments and provide expert support when the employee returns to work. Unfortunately this type of benefit isn't available to freelancers, and without some careful thought and planning, they can find themselves in financial difficulty if an illness hits. And this can be even worse if you have dependants. Like pensions, financial safeguards like life insurance, critical illness cover and so on are often put on to the back burner as you strive to establish and build your freelance career and business. However, just like pensions they're as critical to your future as selling, delivering value to your clients and building your brand, as without them you can find yourself in financial difficulties if you fall ill. The biggest problem is that they take vital cash out of your income and there's no guarantee that you'll ever need them.

So what kinds of cover are out there that you should think about? The most common ones are listed below, but talk to a financial adviser to assess the ones most appropriate for you, and also how much cover you might need.

■ **INCOME REPLACEMENT/INCOME PROTECTION.** These policies provide you with a weekly or monthly sum of money while you're unable to work due to accident or sickness. They fall into two categories: those that pay for one or two years maximum and those that continue to pay out until your chosen retirement age. There are a couple of things to bear in mind. The first is the terms associated with your occupation. Policies can be own occupation which will pay out if you can't follow your current occupation, suited occupation which will pay out if you can't undertake work which for which you could be suited and any occupation if you can't work at all. You need to determine if the policy will continue to pay out if you can undertake jobs outside your own occupation, as some people are caught out by this: they think that they're covered when in fact the insurer assumes that they will be able to perform other roles, and then stops payments. The second is deferment period which can vary from one day to 52 weeks. Deferment period means the time you must be unable to work before they will begin paying benefits. While most employers will pay their employees for a period of time if they're off sick, this isn't the case for the freelancer. So a short deferment is usually more appropriate. In all cases, when you return to work, the policy stops paying and you have to go through the same deferment period for future claims should you need them. Finally, when it comes to insuring against loss of income, you should remember that you can't cover your full earnings. In general, the maximum is between 50 and 65 per cent of your average gross earnings. However, since the payment is tax free, in reality it's much closer to your net pay.

■ **LIFE COVER.** Life policies are the simplest type of protection; you're insuring yourself (or somebody else) for an amount of money to be paid by the insurance company in the event of your (or somebody else's) death. There's very little area for doubt on these policies and they can be useful if you've set up your business with someone else. In the main, policies are relatively inexpensive and have become more affordable over the years, as the population has become healthier and as medical advancements have reduced the chances of dying from major diseases.

- **CRITICAL ILLNESS.** These policies provide cover should you suffer from one of a number of major illnesses, such as cancer. Again, with advances in medical science, fewer of us die when diagnosed with serious conditions such as heart disease. We may, however, have an impaired quality of life and be unable to work, which is why critical illness policies have become more popular. Policies aren't related to any form of treatment, nor do they pay directly for any treatment. They just pay out an agreed sum of money (dependent on the cover you choose), if you're diagnosed with a critical illness. How you choose to spend the money is entirely up to you, although many people decide to seek private care and reduce their outgoings by paying off their mortgage.

Medium-term investing

Having addressed your short-term and long-term needs and protected yourself against those unforeseen events that can scupper any freelance career, the final element to consider is the medium-term savings you should build up.

We live in a society where we can get pretty much whatever we want immediately without too much trouble; that's the upside of credit and it can be very helpful if used wisely. The downside, of course, isn't pleasant and some of the broader economic issues we now face are due to the overspending of already over-burdened consumers (this is especially the case in the US, although the UK isn't far behind). The days of easy credit may be over for the moment, but they probably won't be gone forever. Avoiding the traps associated with it is always a good idea, and this is best achieved by establishing a strategy for medium-term savings.

Medium-term savings are a little like pensions, although you can access the money if you need it. And as you build up your pot, you may choose to invest it in the business at a later date (better than a loan), make a major purchase such as a car, or keep it to augment your retirement savings (which is what I tend to do). And like everything else to do with personal finance, there are some options. There's the building society route as well as the high-interest bank account, but there are other avenues that offer you some additional tax advantages –my favourite is the individual savings account (ISA). An ISA is a tax-advantaged means by which people can invest without incurring income or capital gains tax on the proceeds. An ISA isn't an investment in itself but rather a 'wrapper' that allows you to invest in other assets including cash deposits (building society accounts, unit trusts and some National Savings products); stocks and shares; gilts; overseas investments and life assurance products such as with-profits bonds and unit-linked life insurance funds. An ISA will allow you to invest up to £7,200 on a tax-efficient basis each year. There's no tax relief on money put into ISAs on entry, unlike contributions to a pension scheme. Instead, you aren't liable to pay income or capital gains tax on the proceeds of an ISA and the investments you hold within an ISA grow free of income and capital gains tax. You can invest up to £3,600 in cash leaving a further £3,600 to invest in stocks and shares, or put all your allowance in stocks and shares, if you wish.

As a general rule, when it comes to medium-term investments it's important to balance accessibility with income growth and available tax benefits. And if you have a partner, you can also invest under their name to increase the tax advantages. For example, if your partner doesn't go out to work, you can place surplus income in a building society account under his or her name, as he or she will receive interest gross rather than net of tax.

Bricks and mortar

There's one other area of personal finance that's worth mentioning here and that relates to mortgages.

Traditionally, it's been more difficult for the self-employed to get mortgages because lenders preferred to see the regular income guaranteed by employment. Thankfully this has changed over the years and there are plenty of mortgage lenders who specialise in working with the self-employed. As more people have gone down the self-employment route, many mainstream lenders have also become more comfortable in catering for them. That said, lenders can still be conservative and prefer to see how regular your income is. So if you happen to be a gainfully employed freelance software developer, you're likely to be looked on more favourably than a jobbing actor whose income is likely to be highly erratic.

If you're relatively new to freelancing, securing a mortgage might be difficult until you've established yourself. Equally, if you're on a short-term contract without any options for an extension, the same difficulties might apply. However, if you can show that you've had a succession of contracts which have been extended, then it's likely to be less of an issue. The key is to be able to demonstrate a regular income over an extended period of time, usually a couple of years. Lenders will usually want to see proof of income, and this is more likely as the rules for lending money tighten following the recent credit crunch in which lenders relaxed their rules and lent money to people who couldn't really afford to pay it back. Most expect to see two or three audited accounts from your business, and most will base their lending on the net, not gross income of the business.

One of the common ways to secure a mortgage is to take out a self-certification mortgage. Although anyone is able to take out this kind of mortgage, they're particularly suited to the self-employed who've traditionally found it difficult to secure mortgages, often being refused or offered loans which were too small. The good thing about the self-certification mortgages is that they don't require proof of income, although the lender will probably check that you're able to afford to make payments by confirming this with your accountant, and all will perform a credit check. The only downside – and this is especially true when credit conditions deteriorate – is that some lenders may consider such loans higher risk and will either require a larger deposit or charge a higher interest rate. There is precious little reason for this – recent statistics showed that the number of repossessions on self-certified mortgages is no higher than for other types of mortgage. Finally, as a freelancer, you won't be restricted to what type of mortgage you can take out, although a flexible mortgage will provide some advantage over-repayment and endowment mortgages. These allow you to borrow an agreed amount but with a degree of payment flexibility inbuilt; you'll be able to increase, decrease or in some cases temporarily suspend the mortgage repayments depending on your financial situation.

I've covered a lot of personal finance issues in this chapter and, given the limited space, have only been able to provide you with a summary of each. If nothing else, I hope that this will have spurred you on to consider them in more detail and build similar financial disciplines that you apply to your business. Before moving on to the final chapter, here are my top ten tips for personal finance:

1 set yourself some financial goals and review these on an annual basis, as they'll undoubtedly change as you do. And if you have a partner, it's best to do this planning together;

2 prioritise your savings so that you build up your rainy day fund first; remember cash is still king;

3 seek financial advice from someone who's both qualified and also independent; the personal finance market as well as the rules are moving all the time and you won't have the time to keep on top of it yourself;

4 prepare yourself for unforeseen events by establishing the appropriate safety nets such as critical illness cover and medium-term investments;

5 in terms of saving, if it isn't hurting you're probably not putting enough aside;

6 when your income rises, increase your savings so that you don't get used to having the surplus cash to spend;

7 start your long-term investments as early as you can, and let time work for you;

8 use standing orders and direct debits to take the money out of your account automatically; it won't be long before you treat it as an expense; the discipline is great once you get used to it;

9 live within your means; a surplus at the end of the month is better than a deficit;

10 remember to cut yourself a little slack every now and then and indulge yourself.

And now we can move on to the final chapter, which is all about growth. Although not every freelancer sees themselves heading up a global empire, most of us would like to maintain a good income over the course of our working lives. To do so means developing and honing our skills and planning for the future. So let's see what the freelancer should do.

10 A path to growth

Most of this book addresses what I consider to be the most pressing financial issues facing freelancers. This is, of course, important as we all have to focus on earning a living *today*, something that all freelancers are acutely aware of. But what of *tomorrow*? How well equipped are we to continue to earn a good living five, or perhaps 10, years from now?

Having a strong reputation and being able to deliver solid results are two of the best ways to establish an effective brand and to win repeat work, as we saw in Chapter 5 when we looked at how to source work. Reputation is one of the mainstays of a freelance career. Few of us would last for long without it and whatever industry you work in, you're only as good as your last job. However, relying purely on your reputation to sustain a long-term freelance career isn't enough. It is important to remember that our knowledge attenuates over time and if we do little to maintain the currency of our capabilities then it will be tricky to maintain an income level that would sustain a long-term freelance career.

Clearly there's a range of factors to guard against as you navigate your freelance career, including the impacts of technological change, changing economic conditions and increased competition. However, the biggest threat to freelancers comes from the impacts of commoditisation, mentioned briefly earlier. Commoditisation has the ability to undermine our skills and capabilities and to reduce their value on the open market (remember how the value of a project manager has reduced over time). Keeping ahead of this and the other competitive threats means that freelancers have to develop new skills and capabilities just like any other employee. However, unlike employees who receive training and development courtesy of their employer, freelancers have to manage and pay for this themselves.

Important though it is, there's more to maintaining an effective long-term freelance career than training. Other things such as business planning and developing a range of softer skills – team working, cultural sensitivity and so on – are also important. And as a freelancer, these have to be even more refined because you move from project to project, organisation to organisation and team to team.

So when it comes to underwriting your financial future, I believe there are three areas on which to concentrate:

1   **TRAINING AND DEVELOPMENT** focused on the technical and general business skills you need to continue to be successful as you deliver your services to your clients;

2   **DEVELOPING YOUR SOFTER SKILLS** to enhance your client
    handling and teamworking capabilities and to increase your general
    self-awareness (always a good thing in my mind);

3   **BUSINESS PLANNING** focused on setting a suitable direction for your
    company.

Taken together, these three streams form the foundation
of a long-term freelance career.

Training and development

When it comes to training and development, the freelancer
has to be more discerning than the typical employer. The
training and development most employees receive varies
considerably both in terms of its scope and its relevance.
We've probably all been on courses that were of little or no
use at all, other than affording us a few days out of the office.
We've also probably all been on some excellent ones that
have enhanced our skills, capabilities and self-awareness. It's
a bit hit and miss for employers, then, in terms of return.
When you're paying for the course yourself, though, not
only are you spending your own cash but you're giving up
valuable time too.

If we accept that our ability to earn will depend on our
ability to learn, then as freelancers we should be adopting

an active approach to enhancing our skills and capabilities. What freelancers don't have, of course, is the luxury of a guaranteed pay cheque at the end of the month; they can't just take a week or two out of the office without it having a significant impact on their income. Training will also need to be carefully scheduled around other commitments. So, before you sign up for a course or pick out an improving book to read, it's important to understand what you need in relation to training and a good idea to spend a bit of time thinking about the skills and capabilities you need to develop.

One of the best ways to identify your training and development needs is to use the GROW model. This is designed to draw out what you want to achieve and how you're going to achieve it by stepping through four stages:

- stage 1 is about defining your goals;
- stage 2 is focused on understanding what is happening now in relation to these goals by assessing what you currently know and what you need to know;
- stage 3 helps to explore the variety of options you could take to implement your strategy;
- stage 4 is about taking action. In other words making it happen.

The model is both simple and effective and I'll walk you through each stage in turn.

Stage 1 – identify your goals (the G of the GROW model)

We all have goals in life. Some are well articulated, while others appear fanciful. Many are hidden from view. The important thing about goals is to make them explicit by writing them down. The very process of committing them to paper will create an association in your brain and hence make them more likely to occur. However, setting goals without establishing a course of action to meet them will, in the main, ensure that they remain on paper. The first step is therefore designed to help you understand what your career goals are over the next few years. This is achieved by answering the following questions:

- Where do you see yourself three, five and 10 years from now?
- How will you know when you have achieved your goal?
- What will you see, hear and feel, having achieved your goal?
- What will you know when you have reached this goal?
- How much personal control do you have over your goal?
- What resources do you need to accomplish this goal?

These questions will help you visualise the completion of the goal and help you make it appear real rather than abstract. They'll also help you to assess how you'll get there and what kind of training and development you'll need.

Stage 2 – understand reality and what needs to change (the R of the GROW model)

Having defined your goals, you need to establish where you currently sit in relation to them. In essence, it's about stocktaking on your knowledge and learning. The purpose of this stage is to answer the following questions:

- What do you know at the moment (in the widest sense)?
- What is missing from this?
- What skills and knowledge do you need to develop (based upon the goals you've set yourself)?
- What skills and knowledge do you need to drop?
- What skills and knowledge do you have which you're not currently using, and hence which you can refresh and exploit?

This stage consists of three steps:

1 **CURRENT STATE ASSESSMENT** which involves understanding what skills you currently have;
2 **BLIND-SPOT ANALYSIS** which entails taking a hard look at the gaps in your knowledge;

3 **FUTURE PROFILE ASSESSMENT,** which requires you to identify your
future skill needs.

Current state assessment

This first step is very important as it creates the baseline
from which you can then assess your blind spots and
develop your future profile. Understanding reality should
start by assessing your skills and knowledge levels (low and
high, or somewhere in between). Make a note of all your
skills, both soft and hard, and take a view on how deep
these skills are.

Blind-spot analysis

Once complete, the next thing to do is to assess your
knowledge and use this to help identify your most
significant blind spots. This can be done using the
knowledge grid below.

The grid has four quadrants and you'll have things that
go in each.

■ **EXPLICIT KNOWLEDGE.** These are the things that you know that you
know. You can discuss them in detail and you're comfortable in their
application. It's also easy for you to write them down and explain to
other people. In essence, they're at the forefront of your mind and are
easy to recall. These are probably the things you are known for in your

	I know	I don't know
I know	Explicit knowledge	Knowledge gaps
I don't know	Tacit knowledge	Blind spots

work and are likely to be functional in nature; they may even form the basis of your freelance career, honed through years of experience. This knowledge sits well and truly in your comfort zone

■ **TACIT KNOWLEDGE.** Here you don't know that you know something. Very often you'll perform tasks or apply knowledge automatically. Sometimes such knowledge can be 'lost' and if only occasionally applied can be difficult to regain without some refresher training. This, of course, may be because the knowledge is no longer relevant or is so commonly applied that it requires little thought; in essence a commodity skill which is easily transferable. However, it's still worth checking it out before you finally discard it – just to make sure it's no longer serving you the way it once did

■ **KNOWLEDGE GAPS.** You may already know where the gaps in your knowledge lie and indeed may be actively trying to plug them. Some will be obvious, such as the functional skills you need to acquire and develop in order to progress in your freelance career. Others may fall out from your goal assessment, as these may be things you may have never considered as important to learn until you identified them as a gap. Identifying the gaps in your knowledge is crucial because it's these that will drive your training and development strategy in the short and medium term and will help you capture those aspects of your strategy that will help to protect you from commoditisation

- **BLIND SPOTS.** These are those things you've yet to identify as being necessary for your working life and you'll probably be oblivious to them. We do have to be careful about blind spots because we all have them to a greater or lesser extent. Very often they may be pointed out to us by a third party which makes them all the more difficult to accept, especially if this happens to be your client.

At the end of this assessment, you'll have:

- captured your current skill and knowledge profile;
- assessed your levels of explicit and implicit knowledge;
- highlighted your knowledge gaps.
- identified some and, if you're lucky, all of your blind spots.

Future profile assessment

Having completed your current state assessment, it's now a good idea to develop a future profile which identifies the depth and breadth of skills, and capabilities you need in the future. When creating this second profile you'll need to revisit your goals to ensure this new profile matches them.

Stage 3 – determine your options (the O of the GROW model)

Now that you've completed stages 1 and 2, the next thing to do is to determine what you need to do to close the gap between the current and future states. But rather than jumping straight to action, it's better to explore the wider options first. This stage is therefore designed to answer the following questions:

- What could you do to shift yourself from where you are now to where you want to be (as defined by your goals)?
- What alternatives are available?
- What approaches have you seen used in similar circumstances?
- Who might be able to help?
- What constraints do you have to work within (time, money etc.)?
- If the constraints were removed, what would you do?
- Which of the options interests you?

Stage 4 – action planning or way forward (the W of the GROW model)

This final stage is about action planning which is designed to answer the following questions:

- What are the next steps?
- Will these address your goals?
- When will you take them?
- What might get in the way?
- How will you ensure that the next steps are taken?
- Who needs to know?
- How will you get the support you need?

The GROW model and its principal steps should help you clarify what you want to achieve in your freelance career and, more importantly, take the necessary dispassionate look at your skills and capabilities. If you can commit to this process and to repeating it every 2–3 years, you'll be able to assess where you are along your journey and update it as required. More importantly, it'll allow you to keep a weather eye on how commoditisation is changing the working dynamic and what skills are likely to be in vogue and which ones are likely to become commoditised in the months and years ahead.

Having identified what skills and expertise you might require in the future, you can then determine how best you're going to develop them. There's a wide range of options, including:

- **PUBLIC TRAINING COURSES.** Numerous public courses are available to the freelancer, but those of interest are likely to be open courses in which it's possible to join freelancers and employees from other companies on the same course. These have some distinct benefits because you're able to increase your learning from hearing about other people's experiences. The costs range from as little as a few hundred to thousands of pounds, depending on what you're expecting to learn and whether or not you want to become accredited. For example, many freelancers seek to become accredited in project management and will follow structured courses which lead to a suitable qualification (such as Prince2); the same is true for software engineers who wish to work with Microsoft products (who become certified by following classroom based courses). There can be advantages from becoming accredited and some clients may expect you to have some kind of formal qualification (such as project management).

■ **E-LEARNING.** The Internet today is a huge resource for learning, allowing individuals to share knowledge and learn from others more rapidly than ever before – without having to rely on libraries and printed books. With plenty of sites dedicated to single subjects, chat rooms where it's possible to swap ideas and offer advice, and online universities and learning resources providing distance learning via the Web, expanding knowledge has never been easier for the individual. Moreover, the Internet provides a rich environment that can bring the learning process alive with a mix of graphics, self-assessments, video, audio, and real-time interaction. There are already many e-learning providers that can facilitate your online learning. The beauty of these is that they provide a ready-made environment for learning and can save you enormous amounts of time searching for the relevant material yourself. Here are two: Learning Matters (www.learningmatters.com) and NoonTime University (www.noontimeu.com). Learning Matters is a virtual learning centre that contains over 1,500 resources for the corporate and personal learner. The site offers a wealth of learning solutions including training videos, self-development resources, management articles and case studies, e-based diagnostic and audit solutions and management books. The site is well organised, up to date, and for the self-directed learner reasonably priced. NoonTime University offers educational courses for busy professionals who can't get away from work. This innovative site offers some 40, three-hour, high-impact, tailored courses covering management, administration and more general subjects over lunch periods and early evening. This addresses the common complaint that it can be very difficult to fit in longer training courses in a busy work schedule.

- **ON THE JOB LEARNING.** 'Development' typically conjures up the concept of organised training courses. But in fact 70 per cent of a typical employee's development is while they're doing their normal job. In other words, it's experience and understanding gained during their day-to-day work. This may include some form of mentoring or shadowing but may simply be through working with new people or in different situations or project teams. Carefully chosen freelance roles can also be developmental. The key is finding roles where you're able to deliver and still learn at the same time.

▪ **CYCLES OF EXPERIENCE.** We've all been through distinct cycles of experience during our careers, and these experiences are usually associated with developing and mastering a new skill, moving business sectors or changing employers. These cycles are increasingly critical to us all and it's a good idea to make learning from them an active process. To do so involves following a few simple steps. The first is to focus on what you want to learn, or gain expertise in (which you can do with the GROW model). Once you've decided what you want to achieve, set yourself some objectives that might be associated with a specific experience, like running a large project, a skill you want to acquire through a training course or perhaps a combination of both. You then need to think about how you're going to achieve them. As you pass through the experience, you might want to use an after action review (AAR) every now and then to assess how well you're doing against your targets. The AAR originated during the Vietnam War, where the soldiers in the field knew more than those at headquarters. It allows people to learn immediately after an event, irrespective of whether it was a success or failure. To get the best out of it, you need to answer the following questions:

▪ What should have happened?
▪ What actually happened?

- What were the differences between what should have happened, and what actually happened?
- What lessons can be drawn from the experience and how can any strengths revealed be built upon, and any weaknesses reduced or eliminated?

I find this really helps to track how well you're doing against the objectives you set yourself and provides you with the basis for making adjustments. Once you've achieved your objectives, you can then decide on what your next cycle of experience is going to be. I've found cycles can last from as little as a few months to as much as a few years and the amount of time it takes will depend on the nature of the objectives you set yourself. However long it takes, it's a great way to remain fresh and actively engaged in your freelance career.

- **READING AND SELF-DIRECTED LEARNING.** Books and journals are a ready source of information and knowledge. Both provide you with the opportunity to tap into other people's ideas, best practices and experiences without the need to carry out the research, make the same mistakes or indeed have the same insights as the authors' did. Ultimately, a combination of a good library and subscriptions to the more forward-thinking journals, such as the *Harvard Business Review* make an ideal combination for continuous learning (of course, this depends hugely on the type of freelance work you do, as for some freelancers, this level of reading may be unnecessary). There are a couple of advantages associated with reading and having an extensive library. First, they allow you to develop your ability to connect ideas and concepts together, which is one of the principal ways new ideas are generated. And second, they provide a major source of knowledge and information which you can tap into when you need. So, in the case of the library, you should have books which you'll only dip into to support your work, as well as those which you'll read from cover to cover. The bottom line is that books and journals provide knowledge in a pre-packaged form that, if taken seriously, can enhance your learning many times over. Why develop something from scratch when you can fast track the outcome by building on what's already known?

Developing your softer skills

We're increasingly told by a whole range of experts that our soft skills are just as important as our technical abilities. Although this is generally true, it's important to recognise that most freelancers are hired principally on the basis of their technical capabilities – after all, that's why organisations want to use them. That said, everyone benefits from working with a range of people and organisations from different cultures, so the need to be able to adapt to new situations and to work effectively with different people means that freelancers can't ignore their softer skills.

Although I could probably write an entire book about soft skills, here are two areas that are most relevant to the freelancer, both of which are focused on developing the mindsets that will benefit you as you continue with your freelance career.

Neuro Linguistic Programming (NLP) – building resilience and maintaining your motivation

One of the best ways to gain the flexible mindset you need to be a successful freelancer is to use the principles and techniques of Neuro Linguistic Programming (NLP). NLP was derived from research into the transference of therapy skills between counsellors and since then it's been adopted by business coaches and others who're interested in helping people reach their peak performance. The neuro (N) component states that our behaviour stems from the way we experience the world around us through our five senses. It also relates to our physiological reactions to the things we sense. The linguistic (L) element relates to the language we use to order our thoughts and behaviour, and the way we communicate with those around us. Finally, the programming (P) aspect refers to the way in which we, as individuals, choose to respond to the conditions around us.

There are two elements to NLP that are of particular relevance to freelancers – understanding and changing beliefs and maintaining peak motivation and performance.

The former is about updating our belief system to become more effective. We all have barriers to personal growth that are embedded in the way we view ourselves and these can restrict our perceived capabilities. NLP provides the basis for reframing our self beliefs to become more successful by focusing on how we can adjust to the world around us more effectively. It provides some tools with which to do this including modelling and visualising success, reframing failure as an opportunity to learn, and understanding and adjusting our personal values.

The second element is associated with maintaining peak motivation and performance using our physiology. This essentially means identifying physical feelings, body posture and mental images associated with success, achievement and high performance and replicating these time after time. To give an example, this was how Roger Bannister was able to break the four-minute mile, despite the received wisdom of the medical profession at the time believing it to be impossible and potentially life threatening. More importantly, it means recognising the physiology associated with low performance and either avoiding it, or having recognised it, switching into a more positive, high-performing state. This plays on the well-known fact that the brain's ability to process information is far greater when a person is in a high-performing state than when they are in a low-performing state. It also means that, when in a high-performing state, an individual is more resourceful and more able to overcome significant obstacles. It is worth taking a course on NLP because, if nothing else, it'll provide you with some new techniques which you can use to approach your freelance career and face the inevitable challenges more positively.

Developing future-oriented mindsets – future-proofing your freelance career

Howard Gardner, professor of cognition and education at Harvard Business School, recently published the book *Five Minds for the Future*[1] in which he outlined the cognitive abilities that will command a premium in the coming decades. He believes that the combination of globalisation, increasing amounts of information and the domination and penetration of technology necessitates a new way of thinking in education and business circles. Although Gardner doesn't explicitly mention the nature of freelance work or indeed freelancers, it's clear that the mindsets he introduces can be helpful to use as you address the challenges of a freelance career. The five mindsets are:

[1] Gardner, H. (2006), *Five Minds for the Future*, Boston, Massachusetts: Harvard Business School Press

- **THE DISCIPLINED MIND.** Gardner makes the distinction between knowing facts (and being able to regurgitate these when required) and disciplined thinking. While the former allows people to give the impression of having deep knowledge, it often fails them because they see information as an end in itself. What makes information useful – and indeed the freelancer invaluable – is the ability to use a combination of the wider context within which the information sits and the means to better-informed practice. In other words, Gardener is recommending that we understand our disciplines – be that accounting, marketing or information technology – very well rather than superficially. And he believes that once you delve deeply into a subject, you'll naturally want to find out more, thus creating a virtuous cycle of learning, development and practice.

- **THE SYNTHESISING MIND.** The ability to knit together information from a wide range of sources is increasingly important in today's workplace. And as the amount of information continues to double every two or so years, this mindset will be the one that will command the highest premium. Unfortunately, it's also one of the hardest to master, especially as it requires you to apply the disciplined mindset to multiple subject areas and to see the connections between them. It's also a mindset that's not generally recognised or rewarded in most organisations but is one that's useful for certain areas of freelancing, such as consultancy.

- **THE CREATING MIND.** Corporations everywhere talk of the need to harness the creativity and the innovative capabilities of their employees, yet few seem to be able to do it successfully. The problem is that creative people tend to stand out from the rest of their colleagues (which they usually enjoy), are generally dissatisfied with the status quo and are willing to question and challenge convention. This creates problems for the organisation that requires order, discipline and functional experts. Those who stick out are often marginalised, or in extreme cases fired. This presents a real opportunity for those among the freelance ranks who possess this kind of capability.

- **THE RESPECTFUL MIND.** This may not appear, on face value at least, to be a mindset that'll help you maintain a productive freelance career. But on a second look, developing it could serve you well. However, the need to work effectively with people from different cultures, with diverse life experiences and with different skills and capabilities is critical to a freelancer's survival in the workplace. Therefore, respecting other people both for what they are and for what they bring will be essential if you're going to be respected yourself.

- **THE ETHICAL MIND.** Acting in an ethical way is the bedrock of trust – and trust in the workplace is vital if an organisation's position in the market is to be maintained. One only needs to look back a few years to see how quickly trust can unravel when the leaders of an organisation turn out to be unethical. The demise of Enron, WorldCom, Andersen and the many others who were caught up in the accounting scandals of the early 2000s is testament to the need to remain ethical; markets and authorities are far less forgiving than they used to be. So if you're considered to be ethical, trustworthy and professional, you're more likely to be perceived to be valuable by any organisation.

Although we could argue that it's possible to get by without the need for developing all of the mindsets that Gardner believes are critical, he makes his case for them very strongly when he outlines the downside of not developing them:

- for those who fail to develop one or more of the five disciplines, the future will be bleak, as they'll be unable to cope with the demanding nature of the workplace and will, instead, be restricted to menial tasks and be ideal targets for commoditisation;
- those without the synthesising capabilities will struggle to deal with the ever-increasing amounts of information and data. They'll be overwhelmed with information and will be unable to make effective decisions both in their professional and private lives;
- for those who lack the ability to create, the future will be one of commoditisation with technology replacing their role in the workplace. They'll also drive away those among their ranks who've the creative abilities, which will compound the problems for the broader workplace especially when the premium on innovation will be much higher than it is today;

- those without respect won't be worthy of the same and will infect and destroy the workplace;
- those without ethics will create a workplace devoid of decent workers and, over time, will fail.

Because it's increasingly difficult to predict what we'll be doing in our working life, it's helpful to tap into those who do. I think that Gardener is spot on in terms of what mindsets are likely to be important in the future and although you may not develop each of the mindsets he mentions, I am sure one or two will be critical to your future success as a freelancer.

Another thing to consider when developing your softer skills is coaching. Coaching is increasingly an attractive proposition for busy executives and many organisations now take the trouble to provide mentoring and coaching for their staff, especially those who show potential. It's important to know the difference between coaching and mentoring. Whereas the former is much more active with the coach working through issues with the executive, the latter is more like a sounding board. Second, coaches don't usually have a deep technical knowledge of what you do, they are there to coach not to teach. Their role is to bring out the best from you and to explore ideas with you without the critical eye of the technical expert. Coaching can be a mix of:

- **GENERIC COACHING** (which seeks to provide a general understanding about problems that need resolution and to develop a degree of self-sufficiency within the person being coached especially when it comes to taking action);

- **MENTORING** (which attempts to develop a better understanding of the organisation in which you work, although this can be more widely focused);

- **TUTORING** (which is aimed at increasing someone's competence in a particular discipline, or to widen the breadth of knowledge in the person being coached) and confronting (which deals with the shortfalls in our capabilities and performance).

I've used coaches from time to time, and I know plenty of freelancers who also use them in a targeted way. Used carefully, they can be an enormous help and can be particularly effective in dealing with the difficult issues which arise every so often in a freelance career. If you're considering using a coach, do your research and above all else make sure there's a good fit between you and the coach.

Business planning
The final element that every freelancer needs to consider is business planning. Although this might not seem that

significant, especially if you use agencies or aren't interested in growing your business, there's merit in performing some kind of business-planning exercise every couple of years or so. Of course, if you needed to raise some capital to allow you to start your business, you'd have had to produce a business plan for the bank, in which case it's a good idea to dust it down and update it.

If you haven't produced a business plan before, then as a minimum you would need to:

- outline the market or markets in which your business operates. This could be a specific market such as publishing or IT testing, or more general, such as general business consulting. You might want to include market segments if you want to be more precise, such as IT testing in retail banking for example.
- describe in detail the shape and size of the market in which you operate. This should include information on its overall size, its primary segments, any major trends, the principal drivers and any factors that could drive your clients' priorities and investment decisions.
- detail your existing business as it relates to the markets you've chosen. Here you should include such things as current sales, your clients, your products and services, revenue figures and profits. You should develop different views on this data so that you can make assessments by client as well as by product/service. It's also a good idea to analyse where you're getting most of your revenue, as you may find that the

majority of your business comes from a small number of clients. Such an analysis is important as it could help you target similar organisations rather than chasing every opportunity.

- describe your products and services. This should include a detailed description of the service or product you offer, their unique selling points and the situations in which your clients would buy the product or use the service.

- outline your routes to market. This is likely to include the Internet, the use of agencies, direct selling, other organisations you may involve in the sale or delivery of your product or service and who your target audiences are (for example, CEO, CFO, divisional manager, commissioning editor, newspaper editor and so on). It's important that you're as specific as possible because this will help you really to get to grips with how you approach the sales process. Some freelancers have found it helpful to develop mini-case studies and citations of what they've done in the past – these can be very helpful in articulating the value you deliver to your clients.

- identify your competitors. Although it's best to be as specific as possible, for many freelancers it could be in-house experts (i.e. those with similar skills but employed in the organisations you might be targeting) or other freelancers. If you're able to determine exactly who your competitors are, you could perform a SWOT (strengths, weaknesses, opportunities and threats) assessment against them, as this will help you determine how best to tackle them.

- prepare a detailed summary of your revenues by product/service and client (current and target) for one or two financial years. This should

include such things as cost of sales, revenues, profit margins and
operating costs, and should be phased monthly. In essence, this forms
the budget against which you'll be able to assess how well your
business is doing and to address any variances from your plan.

- list the actions you'll be taking to realise your plan and outline the
effort required to complete them, as this will help you to prioritise your
effort when you aren't busy with your clients. The list can be reviewed
monthly and is helpful way to maintain momentum.

As with everything else financial, it may be a good idea to
seek some professional help either from your bank, your
accountant or a specialist in business planning. At face
value, business planning can seem to be both time
consuming and of limited use to freelancers, but it can be
enlightening. For me, it gives the necessary structure and
rigour that ensures my freelance career isn't some kind of
random walk between clients and assignments. I think a
few hours spent business planning each year pays dividends
later on and I commend it to you.

So, we're now at the end of the book. Over the course of
the last 10 chapters, I've tried to cover a range of issues
which either directly or indirectly impact the finances of a
freelancer. Some of them are comparatively straightforward
to address, while others are a little more complex. However,
taken in the round, they represent pretty much everything

a freelancer should consider. And if you use this book as the foundation for further investigation of the concepts and topics mentioned, then it's served its purpose.

There's no doubt in my mind that being a freelancer takes real courage. It involves making some tough decisions, requires resilience and necessitates high levels of motivation. In the end though, the long-term success of any freelance career requires financial discipline. So, as one freelancer to another, I wish you the best of luck and, as you know as well as I do, no matter how tough it gets, it sure beats working for someone else.

Useful links

The good news is that there are plenty of resources available to the freelancer, and here are a few which I hope you'll find useful. Happy surfing!

- www.hmrc.gov.uk – the best source for anything associated with tax and one of the best places to start when going out on your own
- www.icm.org.uk – The Institute of Credit Management has a useful website for those who want to know a bit more about dealing with credit issues
- www.businesslink.gov.uk – a great site for everything you need to know about running a small business with plenty of helpful resources
- www.companieshouse.gov.uk – the place to go when setting up your company and when you need to understand the legal obligations
- www.fsb.org.uk – another useful site for small businesses. The Federation of Small Businesses is the largest organisation representing small and medium-sized businesses
- www.calculator.co.uk – a great site to help you address the financial aspects of freelancing
- www.icaewfirms.co.uk – The Institute of Chartered Accountants website is the best site to find an accountant

Also by Andrew Holmes

Business

Failsafe IS Project Delivery (Aldershot: Gower Publishing); 2001

Smart Things to Know About Technology Management (Chichester: Capstone); 2003

The Chameleon Consultant: Culturally Intelligent Consulting (Aldershot: Gower Publishing); 2002

ExpressExec Risk Management (Chichester: Capstone); 2001

Smart Things to Know About Risk Management (Chichester: Capstone); 2004

ExpressExec Lifelong Learning (Chichester: Capstone); 2001

Smart Things to Know About Lifelong Learning (Chichester: Capstone); 2003

Commoditization and the Strategic Response (Aldershot: Gower Publishing); 2008

Selling with Confidence: Finding and Closing Successful Deals Without Breaking the Bank (London: A&C Black); 2008

Blowback in Business: How to Avoid Unintended and Undesired Consequences in Decision-Making (Aldershot: Gower Publishing); 2009

Non-fiction

Pass Your Exams: Study Skills for Success (Oxford: Infinite Ideas); 2005

How Much?! A Miscellany of Money Madness (London: Thorogood); 2007

Humour

Pains on Trains: A Commuter's Guide to the 50 Most Irritating Travel Companions (Chichester: Capstone); 2003

Pains in the Office: 50 People You Absolutely, Definitely Must Avoid at Work (Chichester: Capstone); 2004

Pains in Public: The 50 People Most Likely to Drive You Completely Nuts (Chichester: Capstone); 2004

Index